Maria Rosa Poggio

W9-DBL-481

CALL AND MISSION

THE ADVENTURE OF THE TWELVE CONTINUES

Libreria Editrice Vaticana

Illustrations: Casa Artistica, Turin

Photos: 123RF, iStock, Corbis, Getty Images, Blend Images, Lightstock

Iconographic research: Maria Stefania Bruno

ISBN 978-1-60137-439-4

First printing, August 2014

TABLE OF CONTENTS

THE PURPOSE OF THIS BOOK

"I want you, yes, you, not somebody else. I have called you to life by name, and now I call you by name to entrust you with an important and special 'mission possible': to proclaim my Gospel and to serve your brothers and sisters in love and truth."

In many pages of the Gospel, it seems that Jesus wants to address each of us with these words. There are in fact many texts from the Gospel and the New Testament dedicated to the calling of various individuals, Jesus' encounters with them, his entrusting of his mission to them, and their service in love and truth. I have selected the most important and significant texts on these issues and had them illustrated in a modern style rather than a traditional one.

To help you better understand the words of Jesus, the living Word of God, I have briefly contextualized the biblical passage and have commented on it in a simple way so that you can interact as personally as possible with the passage and the Revelation of Jesus. I have suggested brief points for reflection that are best developed in a group. Finally, I have added some selections from the *Catechism of the Catholic Church* and teachings from Pope Benedict XVI and Pope Francis. As you probably know, Jesus called his young disciples by name when he chose them and gave them a plan and a mission. Among these disciples, the Twelve, who were the closest to him, were invested with the responsibility of being pillars of his Church. They were a small group destined for an extraordinary adventure: to spread the Gospel of salvation through the world, proclaiming the crucified and risen Christ.

When Jesus calls them, they do not yet know the amazing experience they are about to begin, but they understand that Jesus is a special person who is able to change their lives with a single glance. They follow him for years; they enthusiastically accompany him on his entrance into Jerusalem but then abandon him during the sorrowful night at Gethsemene.

After Jesus' Resurrection and after Pentecost, they courageously proclaim Jesus as the Son of God and his Gospel of salvation. Many in their old age will be prepared to give their lives for Christ, to testify to his Gospel and to their faith in him, the Son of God, and to his Resurrection. In the following pages, I want to call your attention to some episodes in which Jesus of Nazareth is the primary protagonist. They involve disciples and Apostles, enthusiastic young people and adults, who will in time be bold witnesses of the Gospel. The Twelve will be the agents of the evangelization that spread Christianity in the space of a single generation to the four corners of the known world of their day. Since that time, the Church has tirelessly continued this mission, proclaiming the Gospel, baptizing new believers, administering the sacraments, and serving every generation throughout the world in love.

This extraordinary mission is not over yet! The adventure of the Apostles continues today, with each of you, with all of you. Jesus still calls young apostles by name today, saying, "I want you!"

Maria Rosa Poggio

BRIEF USER'S GUIDE

To distinguish the different parts of the book that accompany the biblical passages, we have organized things this way:

The title indicates the topic, the leading theme we will focus on.

The **biblical passage** is set against a yellow background. The text is not always cited in its entirety. For better comprehension, however, it is best to read the whole passage to familiarize yourself with the Word of God.

When the symbol **G** appears, you will find glossary explanations to help you understand specific terms.

Individual Encounters with Jesus

THE RICH YOUNG MAN

Lk 18:18–30

An official asked him this question, "Good teacher, what must I do to inherit eternal life?" Jesus answered him, "Why do you call me good? No one is good but God alone. You know the commandments, 'You shall not commit adultery; you shall not kill; you shall not steal; you shall not bear false witness; honor your father and your mother.'" And he replied, "All of these I have observed from my youth." When Jesus heard this he said to him, "There is still one thing left for you: sell all that you have and distribute it to the poor, and you will have a treasure in heaven. Then come, follow me." But when he heard this he became quite sad, for he was very rich.

Jesus looked at him [now sad] and said, "How hard it is for those who have wealth to enter the kingdom of God! For it is easier for a camel to pass through the eye of a needle than for a rich person to enter the kingdom of God." Those who heard this said, "Then who can be saved?" And he said, "What is impossible for human beings is possible for God." Then Peter said, "We have given up our possessions and followed you." He said to them, "Amen, I say to you, there is no one who has given up house or wife or brothers or parents or children for the sake of the kingdom of God who will not receive [back] an overabundant return in this present age and eternal life in the age to come."

36

The **CONTEXT** of the Passage has information concerning the customs and habits of Jesus' time. Knowing these details is important because it helps us interpret Jesus' actions and words in the correct way.

Your **INTERACTION** with the Text is a careful rereading, almost verse by verse, of the biblical passage being considered. It is fundamental that you to learn how to do this kind of analysis of Scripture so that you do not stop at first impressions and stereotypes but move forward to the actual message the authors wanted to communicate.

The **CONTEXT** of the Passage — This parable refers to an experience that everyone in Israel might have had, namely, planting seed. The parable does not deal with large plots of land on the Galilean plain but with small fields on hillsides full of thorn bushes and brambles that ate still seen near Capernaum, the city where Jesus lived for a while and where Peter's house is located. At one time, seeds were very scarce. To get them, farmers needed to give up part of the harvest from the previous year or to buy them, and no good farmer would have ever wasted any seed. However, even with careful planting, it was impossible for all the seed to end up in good soil because the texture of the soil could be poor.

Your **INTERACTION** with the Text — We have two other versions of this parable (see Mt 13:1–9; Mk 4:1–9). The descriptive details of the agricultural terrain in all versions line up with the real situation at that time. Luke simplifies the story. His reference to the Word of God is clear (v. 11), and the Word becomes a protagonist in this parable. The one who comes to oppose the Word of God is the Devil (v. 12), who carries it out of the hearts of those who had accepted it. In these verses, Luke describes everyday life with the difficulties that Christians can encounter when they accept the Gospel and put into practice all that this entails. The parable likewise speaks of the work that needs to be done concerning the Word of God and its practical and fruitful actualization.

Rereading the Text Together

At the beginning of his work, the farmer does not know how things will turn out, but he continues to plant seed and wait for it to germinate and grow.

In a similar way, willing people can have the seed of the Word of God inside themselves that builds up the Kingdom of God as it ripens and matures. This happens above all through people's acceptance of God's love, which is then reciprocated by a desire to do his will in freedom and righteousness.

But in order for the Word of God to develop, the soil needs to be fruitful. It is people's responsibility to "plow" their own hearts little by little and remove the inner rocks, weeds, and other obstacles. It is not enough for the sower to scatter seed; it is necessary to do so in suitable soil. If the seed does not fall on fertile ground, it might still begin to germinate, but eventually the plant will dry up.

24

The section called **The Protagonists**, with a yellow background, looks at the people in the biblical texts and tries to understand their personalities and their spiritual growth or regression. As we identify with them, we can learn to understand our own attitudes toward Jesus.

The section called **Rereading the Text Together**, with a green background, is a closer reflection on the Scripture passage. After having learned some cultural details and what close analysis can offer, we are now in a position to look at that passage again and draw conclusions that we can use to meditate on concerning the theme in the title.

The section called For Reflection Together, with a blue background, aims to help us apply the message today.

The section called For Deeper Reflection includes selections from the *Catechism of the Catholic Church* or texts from Pope Benedict XVI and Pope Francis. These selections help us more easily see the continuity between the teaching of Scripture and the teachings of the Church.

The Calling of the Twelve

Lk 5:1–11, 27–28, 6:12–16

While the crowd was pressing in on Jesus and listening to the word of God, he was standing by the Lake of Gennesaret. He saw two boats there alongside the lake; the fishermen had disembarked and were washing their nets. Getting into one of the boats, the one belonging to Simon, he asked him to put out a short distance from the shore. Then he sat down and taught the crowds from the boat. After he had finished speaking, he said to Simon, "Put out into deep water and lower your nets for a catch." Simon said in reply, "Master, we have worked hard all night and have caught nothing, but at your command I will lower the nets." When they had done this, they caught a great number of fish and their nets were tearing. They signaled to their partners in the other boat to come to help them. They came and filled both boats so that they were in danger of sinking. When Simon Peter saw this, he fell at the knees of Jesus and said, "Depart from me, Lord, for I am a sinful man." For astonishment at the catch of fish they had made seized him and all those with him, and likewise James and John, the sons of Zebedee, who were partners of Simon. Jesus said to Simon, "Do not be afraid; from now on you will be catching men." When they brought their boats to the shore, they left everything and followed him. . . .

After this he went out and saw a tax collector named Levi [Matthew] sitting at the customs post. He said to him, "Follow me." And leaving everything behind, he got up and followed him. . . .

In those days he departed to the mountain to pray, and he spent the night in prayer to God. When day came, he called his disciples to himself, and from them he chose Twelve, whom he also named apostles: Simon, whom he named Peter, and his brother Andrew, James, John, Philip, Bartholomew, Matthew, Thomas, James the son of Alphaeus, Simon who was called a Zealot, and Judas the son of James, and Judas Iscariot, who became a traitor.

The Protagonists

JESUS is the main protagonist. His actions and words are decisive. He uses imperative verbs: "put out into deep water," "lower your nets," "do not be afraid," and "follow me!" It is Jesus who decides to give the title of Apostles to the **Twelve**.

THE TWELVE generally provide a context for making Jesus' great uniqueness emerge, and in this case, they also demonstrate the extraordinary character of the event they are living through. They have doubts, they try to move ahead, they speak among themselves, they are amazed, they are fearful, but they decide, even in Matthew's case, to follow Jesus.

For Deeper Reflection

Jesus is the Father's Emissary. From the beginning of his ministry, he "called to him those whom he desired. . . . And he appointed twelve, whom also he named apostles, to be with him, and to be sent out to preach" (Mk 3:13–14). From then on, they would also be his "emissaries" (Greek *apostoloi*). In them, Christ continues his own mission: "As the Father has sent me, even so I send you" (Jn 20:21). The apostles' ministry is the continuation of his mission; Jesus said to the Twelve: "he who receives you receives me" (Mt 10:40).

Catechism of the Catholic Church, no. 858

For Reflection Together

Read the passage attentively.

- Try to interpret the passage for today and respond to it. Who is Jesus calling? Who is being addressed? Who should be fishers of men today?

The CONTEXT of the Passage

The Lake of Gennesaret (also called the Lake or Sea of Galilee) has always been a very plentiful source of fish. In Jesus' time, the fishing business was flourishing there. Fishermen at that time used casting nets and dragnets. It seems that there were at least twenty-five kinds of fish in this lake, including a fish now called the St. Peter fish that is bony and hard to eat! Capernaum, on the shore of this lake, was St. Peter's city and probably the place where Matthew had his customs post for tax collection. In Jesus' time, it was thriving city.

The tax collectors, the publicans, assessed the money that was due from a village or a city for the coffers of the Roman emperors. They would then collect the taxes and usually increase the amount due, keeping the overpayment as personal earnings. The Jews hated them because they worked for the despised government of Rome and were making people pay more than they owed.

The Lake of Galilee is mentioned several times in the Gospels.

This was the workplace for the fishermen from among whom Jesus chose Peter, his brother Andrew, James, and John (see Lk 5:1–11).

One day, an unexpected storm arose, putting Jesus and the Apostles in danger. A weary Jesus was sleeping, but the Apostles woke him up, and with a few words, he calmed the fury of the wind and the waves (see Lk 8:22–25 on p. 30).

According to John, who presents a very similar episode to the one in Luke's Gospel, the Lake of Galilee is also the location of one of Jesus' appearances. The disciples were very tired from having fished all night and not having caught anything. Jesus urged them to cast their nets on the other side of the boat. The disciples then caught a large quantity of fish, and through this unusual incident, they recognized this unknown person: "It is the Lord!" (Jn 21:7).

Galilee

Galilee is one of the three regions, in addition to Samaria and Judea, into which the ancient land of Palestine was subdivided. Ancient Galilee existed in its northernmost region, bordering on what is today Lebanon. It is a very fertile region where grapes, olives, barley, flax, and wheat were once grown. One of the geographical characteristics of Galilee is the Lake of Galilee, which is known by multiple names: the Lake of Gennesaret, the Sea of Galilee, the Lake of Tiberias, and Kinneret (meaning "harp" because of its shape as seen on the map). This lake is formed by the river Jordan and is located between the territory of Israel and the Golan Heights in a depression that is around 656 feet below sea level.

Unlike the Dead Sea, this lake is a fresh-water lake well stocked with fish.

For Deeper Reflection

- Some of the facts reported here come from chapters 5 and 6 of Luke's Gospel. To understand what is happening, it is important that you read that whole section.

In chapter 5, verses 1–3, Luke tells us where the story takes place. We are in the area around Lake Gennesaret. We know from archeological study and research that Peter lived in Capernaum, a fishing area. Jesus, who has a special plan for some of the fishermen, offers them a sign that is meaningful to them and that makes his calling of them credible. The account of the miraculous catch of fish is very similar to an episode in John's Gospel (see Jn 21:3–11), and Mark records the calling of Simon (see Mk 1:17–20). In verse 8, Luke uses the name "Simon Peter," even though the second name "Peter" will not be given to him until some time later. In verse 10, Andrew is not named. Jesus, surely surprising his disciples, calls Levi (Matthew) to be one of the Twelve, and Matthew accepts.

Luke's Gospel often shows us Jesus praying. Before selecting the Twelve from among his disciples, Jesus spends the night in prayer because the selection of Apostles is not a light matter. The ones who will be chosen will have a particular mission. They will be Apostles and will have the task of transmitting the Gospel and of being witnesses to all that Jesus said and did.

Ⓖ *Apostolos* is a Greek word that means a person who is commissioned, sent, dispatched. It is found primarily in the texts of the New Testament, where the word indicates more specifically a disciple who is sent to communicate the Gospel, the Good News of the Resurrection of Jesus. Jesus personally chose the disciples who then became Apostles. They are a group that was particularly close to Jesus. Jesus chose twelve of them, a symbolic number that recalls the number of the heads of the twelve tribes of Israel.

"Miracle" is from a Latin word that means "something amazing." A miracle is an extraordinary event performed by God as a sign for human beings. Jesus performs miracles to help people understand that God is the Father, the Lord of Life, and that he himself is the Messiah. The sign can be a gesture, action, or word that helps people understand something mysterious. In this case, the sign-miracle of the catch in Luke is closely tied to the selection of the Twelve. Jesus' intention is that the event will help them understand what their mission will be, namely, to be fishers of men.

Rereading the Text Together

At the beginning of his ministry, Jesus selects certain men to follow him. He does not send out a general call for people to follow him; he always directly addresses people and addresses them as individuals. Before asking them to follow him, Jesus asks some Galilean fishermen to do something they know very well how to do. He does not ask them to do something exceptional or extraordinary; he asks them to cast their nets.

▶

- **Simon,** an experienced fisherman, protests. He has cast his nets all night without any success. Now, here comes the son of a carpenter, who is telling them what they should do! Nevertheless, they cast their nets, and the catch is miraculous. There are so many fish that the nets almost rip.

  The quantity of fish makes Simon Peter, who is a realistic man, aware that he is standing before a man unlike any other, a man who could change the laws of nature and who could ensure a catch of fish that was not possible earlier. Because of the abundance of fish, Peter and his companions understand that Jesus is someone important who is worthy of being followed.

  Jesus is very direct. He tells Peter, "You will be catching men," and he is even more direct with Matthew when he says, "Follow me." Jesus is saying, "Yes, you. I am not talking to somebody else." What Jesus says cannot be misunderstood. Jesus wants each of them: Simon, Matthew, and the others who will form the group of the Twelve. They will be the first "laborers," the first fishers of men in service to the Kingdom of God. Let us look at each of them more closely so we can get to know them.

- **Peter.** His real name is Simon, son of Jonah. Originally from Bethsaida, he is a fisherman. He owns a boat with his brother Andrew, and they fish on the Sea of Galilee. He has a strong character and is full of energy passion, but he is sometimes impetuous. Jesus calls him "Cephas," which means "rock."

- **Andrew.** A brother of Peter, he is among the people closest to Jesus. Together with Peter, he is the first to be called by Jesus to be an Apostle.

- **James and John.** Sons of Zebedee, they also fish the waters of the Sea of Galilee. Because of their lively character, Jesus calls them "sons of thunder"! John is the youngest of the Apostles and will be Jesus' favorite.

- **Philip and Bartholomew (Nathanael).** Philip, like Peter and Andrew, is originally from Bethsaida, and Nathanael is one of his friends. These two are also among the first ones Jesus calls to be with him.

- **Levi (Matthew).** He is probably the richest of the Twelve. When Jesus calls him, he is working at his customs post collecting taxes.

- **Thomas.** He will be the protagonist in the famous episode after the Resurrection of Jesus. Thomas is absent when the risen Jesus appears to the Apostles for the first time, and he does not believe his companions. He says he wants to put his finger in the wounds of Jesus to verify that it is truly him. Seven days later, Jesus satisfies him.

- **James, son of Alphaeus.** He is also known as "James the Less" to distinguish him from John's brother. After the Death and Resurrection of Jesus, he will be the head of the first Christian community in Jerusalem (see Acts 15:13 ff.).

- **Simon.** He is called a "Zealot" because he belonged to a religious group that wanted to have the Romans leave Israel.

- **Judas Thaddeus.** According to tradition, he was one of Jesus' relatives, like James, the son of Alphaeus.

- **Judas Iscariot.** This Apostle is remembered chiefly for his betrayal of the Master. According to an ancient tradition, he was entrusted with the money purse for the Twelve and was in charge of the savings and donations that provided for the needs of Jesus and his Apostles.

The Mission of the Twelve

Mt 10:1–16

Then he summoned his twelve disciples and gave them authority over unclean spirits to drive them out and to cure every disease and every illness. The names of the twelve apostles are these: first, Simon called Peter, and his brother Andrew; James, the son of Zebedee, and his brother John; Philip and Bartholomew, Thomas and Matthew the tax collector; James, the son of Alphaeus, and Thaddeus; Simon the Cananean, and Judas Iscariot who betrayed him.

Jesus sent out these twelve after instructing them thus, "Do not go into pagan territory or enter a Samaritan town. Go rather to the lost sheep of the house of Israel. As you go, make this proclamation: 'The kingdom of heaven is at hand.' Cure the sick, raise the dead, cleanse lepers, drive out demons. Without cost you have received; without cost you are to give. Do not take gold or silver or copper for your belts; no sack for the journey, or a second tunic, or sandals, or walking stick. The laborer deserves his keep. Whatever town or village you enter, look for a worthy person in it, and stay there until you leave. As you enter a house, wish it peace. If the house is worthy, let your peace come upon it; if not, let your peace return to you. Whoever will not receive you or listen to your words—go outside that house or town and shake the dust from your feet. Amen, I say to you, it will be more tolerable for the land of Sodom and Gomorrah on the day of judgment than for that town.

"Behold, I am sending you like sheep in the midst of wolves; so be shrewd as serpents and simple as doves."

For Deeper Reflection

From the beginning of his public life Jesus chose certain men, twelve in number, to be with him and to participate in his mission. He gives the Twelve a share in his authority and "sent them out to preach the kingdom of God and to heal" (Lk 9:2). They remain associated forever with Christ's kingdom, for through them he directs the Church.

Catechism of the Catholic Church, no. 551

For Reflection Together

- We discover in this passage that Jesus' mission is once again addressed to individual people. Jesus decides to choose a group of twelve men who are each named, and he forms a relationship with each of them, entrusting them with a very specific mission. Jesus has a mission for every person, so no believer can say he or she is forgotten. What mission do you think you have?
- Jesus explains very clearly to the Apostles what he wants them to do. First of all, they should preach the Kingdom of God, and then they should imitate him by healing, cleansing lepers, and raising the dead. Christian faith is actually not constituted only by truth that must be believed; it is something that needs to be lived out every day. How do you think you can personally put this into practice?
- The Apostles left to their successors the same tasks they took on with Christ. Therefore, bishops must preach the Gospel while teaching the Church, administering the sacraments, and overseeing communities. The task of believers is to follow their bishops. How do you think the People of God are doing in this regard?
- Today, we no longer find it necessary to shake the dust off our sandals—the dust of the land that is not holy—because Christians do not believe that there is any unholy land. Nevertheless, it is good to remember that it is easy to become entangled in the logic of those who do not believe in Jesus Christ. What do you think? In what way do Christians sometimes let themselves be influenced by thinking, mindsets, and lives that do not conform to Jesus' teaching?

In this passage, we read about the selection of the Apostles. This list was handed down to us in four forms (in Matthew, Luke, Mark, and Acts of the Apostles). The specific names used for the Apostles sometimes vary, and they are mentioned in different orders.

The text says in verse 6 that the first people who should receive the proclamation of salvation are the Jews. To make sense of this, we need to remember that Matthew's Gospel is the one that contains the most references to Jewish culture, most probably because the community he is writing for is primarily composed of Jewish believers. Those who should be contacted first are the lost sheep of Israel. In the Old Testament Israel is presented as a flock that God shepherds, and the Apostles need to go in search of its lost members. The Samaritans were considered heretics by the Jews and thus as unclean people who should be shunned.

Verse 12 refers to the Eastern custom of wishing peace to someone when a house is entered. The peace referred to in the Bible is something concrete. The Hebrew greeting *shalom* includes the fullness of every blessing and not just the absence of war. To wish peace to someone means blessing the house and its inhabitants so that they would overflow with everything that is good and useful. This greeting was effective, and if it was not received by the person to whom it was addressed, it returned to the one who had pronounced it. Verse 14 notes the need to shake the dust off one's feet, the dust of the houses and cities that did not receive the missionaries and their message. Jews thought that the only holy and clean land was that of Israel. The dust of all other places was unclean, and therefore, to dirty one's feet meant to be contaminated. In this case, it is the land of those who do not accept the proclamation of the Apostles that is considered unclean. Perhaps the author also intends to describe how the preaching of the missionaries was received after the Resurrection.

Jesus gave clear instructions to the Apostles: preach, heal the sick, raise the dead, cleanse the lepers, cast out demons. In other words, the mission of the Apostles was to imitate the work of Jesus very closely. The missionaries, as indicated in verses 9–10, need to live in simplicity. They should not take silver or gold, sandals, a sack for the journey, or a walking stick because they have a right to what they need but to nothing more. The proclamation of the Gospel needs to be done for free. Jesus' teaching on this was actually different than that of other masters who insisted on payment for their instruction.

Rereading the Text Together

In this text we again have a list of names, twelve names that represent the apostolic college testified to by the first Christian community. As always, it involves a ▶

personal calling because Jesus does not commission an anonymous, generic group. Faith is entrusted to a person who should feel personally called and sent. The Apostles are asked to take Jesus' place and follow his example.

As missionaries, they have the right to receive their sustenance, but their lives should be simple. What was freely given to them—the proclamation and salvation accepted by faith—should be given freely to all human beings according to Jesus' example.

The mission entrusted by Jesus needs to be widespread and go from city to city and house to house. Obviously, this message is not just for the House of Israel but must be brought to everyone. Missionaries must not stay involved with those who do not accept their preaching. "Shaking the dust off" means that missionaries should not yield to the temptation of compromising themselves with those who do not adhere to the message; they should not yield to the thinking of those who do not want to believe and instead stand firm with the truth of the Gospel.

For Deeper Reflection

But what does living Holy Week mean to us? What does following Jesus on his journey to Calvary on his way to the Cross and the Resurrection mean? In his earthly mission, Jesus walked the roads of the Holy Land; he called twelve simple people to stay with him, to share his journey and to continue his mission. He chose them from among the people full of faith in God's promises. He spoke to all without distinction: the great and the lowly, the rich young man and the poor widow, the powerful and the weak; he brought God's mercy and forgiveness; he healed, he comforted, he understood; he gave hope; he brought to all the presence of God who cares for every man and every woman, just as a good father and a good mother care for each one of their children.

God does not wait for us to go to him but it is he who moves toward us, without calculation, without quantification. That is what God is like. He always takes the first step, he comes toward us.

Jesus lived the daily reality of the most ordinary people: he was moved as he faced the crowd that seemed like a flock without a shepherd; he wept before the sorrow that Martha and Mary felt at the death of their brother, Lazarus; he called a publican to be his disciple; he also suffered betrayal by a friend. In him God has given us the certitude that he is with us, he is among us. "Foxes," he, Jesus, said, "have holes, and birds of the air have nests, but the Son of man has nowhere to lay his head" (Mt 8:20). Jesus has no house, because his house is the people, it is we who are his dwelling place, his mission is to open God's doors to all, to be the presence of God's love.

Pope Francis, General Audience
St. Peter's Square, March 27, 2013

Requirements of Apostolic Life

Mt 8:18–22, 19:27–30

When Jesus saw a crowd around him, he gave orders to cross to the other side. A scribe approached and said to him, "Teacher, I will follow you wherever you go." Jesus answered him, "Foxes have dens and birds of the sky have nests, but the Son of Man has nowhere to rest his head." Another of [his] disciples said to him, "Lord, let me go first and bury my father." But Jesus answered him, "Follow me, and let the dead bury their dead." . . .

Then Peter said to him in reply, "We have given up everything and followed you. What will there be for us?" Jesus said to them, "Amen, I say to you that you who have followed me, in the new age, when the Son of Man is seated on his throne of glory, will yourselves sit on twelve thrones, judging the twelve tribes of Israel. And everyone who has given up houses or brothers or sisters or father or mother or children or lands for the sake of my name will receive a hundred times more, and will inherit eternal life. But many who are first will be last, and the last will be first."

For Deeper Reflection

The renewal of the Church is also achieved through the witness offered by the lives of believers: by their very existence in the world, Christians are called to radiate the word of truth that the Lord Jesus has left us. The Council itself, in the Dogmatic Constitution *Lumen Gentium*, said this: While "Christ, 'holy, innocent and undefiled' (Heb 7:26) knew nothing of sin (cf. 2 Cor 5:21), but came only to expiate the sins of the people (cf. Heb 2:17), . . . the Church . . . clasping sinners to its bosom, at once holy and always in need of purification, follows constantly the path of penance and renewal. The Church, 'like a stranger in a foreign land, presses forward amid the persecutions of the world and the consolations of God,' announcing the cross and death of the Lord until he comes (cf. 1 Cor 11:26). But by the power of the risen Lord it is given strength to overcome, in patience and in love, its sorrow and its difficulties, both those that are from within and those that are from without, so that it may reveal in the world, faithfully, although with shadows, the mystery of its Lord until, in the end, it shall be manifested in full light" (*Lumen Gentium*, no. 8).

Pope Benedict XVI
Apostolic Letter *Porta Fidei*, no. 6

The Proclamation
of the Kingdom

THE PARABLES OF THE KINGDOM

Mt 22:1–14

Jesus again in reply spoke to them in parables, saying, "The kingdom of heaven may be likened to a king who gave a wedding feast for his son. He dispatched his servants to summon the invited guests to the feast, but they refused to come. A second time he sent other servants, saying, 'Tell those invited: "Behold, I have prepared my banquet, my calves and fattened cattle are killed, and everything is ready; come to the feast."' Some ignored the invitation and went away, one to his farm, another to his business. The rest laid hold of his servants, mistreated them, and killed them. The king was enraged and sent his troops, destroyed those murderers, and burned their city. Then he said to his servants, 'The feast is ready, but those who were invited were not worthy to come. Go out, therefore, into the main roads and invite to the feast whomever you find.' The servants went out into the streets and gathered all they found, bad and good alike, and the hall was filled with guests. But when the king came in to meet the guests he saw a man there not dressed in a wedding garment. He said to him, 'My friend, how is it that you came in here without a wedding garment?' But he was reduced to silence. Then the king said to his attendants, 'Bind his hands and feet, and cast him into the darkness outside, where there will be wailing and grinding of teeth.' Many are invited, but few are chosen."

For Deeper Reflection

Jesus' invitation to enter his kingdom comes in the form of *parables*, a characteristic feature of his teaching. Through his parables he invites people to the feast of the kingdom, but he also asks for a radical choice: to gain the kingdom, one must give everything. Words are not enough, deeds are required. The parables are like mirrors for man: will he be hard soil or good earth for the word? What use has he made of the talents he has received? Jesus and the presence of the kingdom in this world are secretly at the heart of the parables. One must enter the kingdom, that is, become a disciple of Christ, in order to "know the secrets of the kingdom of heaven" (Mt 13:11). For those who stay "outside," everything remains enigmatic (Mk 4:11).

Catechism of the Catholic Church, no. 546

To convey his teaching, Jesus chose to use parables, a literary genre that was also used by the rabbis at that time. To explain a difficult or little-known concept, the Master would compare it in a parable to something known to his listeners. Jesus placed the Kingdom of God at the center of his teaching. The Jews were waiting for the time when God would reign over Israel, but they had misunderstood what the Old Testament Prophets had told them in this case.

The Protagonists

THE MAIN PROTAGONIST IS THE KING who is giving a great banquet for his son's wedding and invites all the important people to celebrate with him.

THE SON is fleetingly mentioned. He is the one whose wedding is being prepared; this is the wedding of the Messiah.

THE SERVANTS fulfill the will of the king. These servants are the Old Testament Prophets.

THE KING'S TROOPS are the ones who destroy the city.

THE GUESTS WHO ARE INVITED to the wedding banquet but are unwilling to participate because they are involved in their own affairs are unworthy guests. From the beginning to the end of this parable, they continue to be unworthy and ungrateful for the honor bestowed on them by the king. Some of them even feel justified in insulting and killing the king's servants to avoid being pestered by them. As characters, they develop negatively. They do not speak and we know nothing of them, except that they received an honor they did not know how to handle. The guests are the Jews.

THE PEOPLE are the ones found in the highways. There are good and bad people in this group. Although the previously invited guests were unworthy because they would not even come to the wedding, even in this new group, some are not faultless: one of them is confronted about coming to the feast in inappropriate clothes. The people are all those to whom the Gospel is addressed who should show themselves to be worthy of the invitation.

For Reflection Together

- The quality that many people in this parable have in common is unworthiness. The guests who were first invited are unworthy, but so is the one who goes to the wedding wearing inappropriate garments. The theme of the Last Judgment is often set aside today because people prefer to highlight the honor God will bestow on each individual who decides to become a Christian. We need to remember, though, that honor carries a duty with it. This means that whoever is called to intimacy with God and to participation in the wedding feast of the Son must act in such a way as to respect the dignity of that honor. If you look around today, in what ways can a Christian behave in an unworthy manner?
- In the parable, the king's servants are insulted and killed. There are still today missionaries who are put to death and persecuted as Christians. When persecution is not physical, which is perhaps the majority of the time, persecution can involve mocking. Can you give an example of that? What do you think about that? What should a Christian's attitude be about that?

Matthew 22:1–14 presents the parable of the guests invited to a wedding. The author has probably combined two parables, one about a wedding banquet and one about wedding garments. In addition, he has added two verses (vv. 11–13) that seem to come from the parable of the wicked tenants, perhaps as a reference to the destruction of Jerusalem.

Being invited to a wedding has always been a great honor, and that was true for the Jews in Jesus' time. Marriage was very important because it meant the beginning of a family, which was considered fundamental to society. The importance of a marital relationship is testified to in the Old Testament by the theme of God as the bridegroom and Israel as the bride. The covenant established with Israel recalls a wedding too: tradition holds that after the covenant was given at Sinai, the elders of Israel ate with God and, instead of perishing, lived.

The image of the banquet also calls to mind the messianic time in which people will be fully able to enjoy the presence of Israel's true king, God, which includes being "invited to his table." In the Bible, the image of a feast is a symbol of the messianic wedding (see Is 25:6–9; Mt 8:11, 26:29; Lk 14:15; Rev 19:9, 17). In this parable, a king invites many people to the wedding feast of his son, but they snub his invitation. The king is God himself, and we can interpret the wedding feast as the blessed state that people will enjoy in the messianic age.

The son of the king for whom the banquet is held is Jesus, who is also the Messiah. The servants who are initially sent to bring the guests are both the Prophets of the Old Testament and the Apostles, the prophets of the New Covenant. These servants do the work of announcing the invitation, an invitation that can go unheeded and can even become dangerous for the servants. The guests who prefer the humdrum affairs of daily life are the unworthy Jews. They even end up killing the Prophets.

The second group of invited guests is composed of pagans and sinners. The city destroyed by the king's troops is Jerusalem, which will be razed to the ground by the Romans in AD 70.

A scene shift starts in verse 11. We are no longer only at a wedding feast, and we learn that a judgment will take place. The Last Judgment is on the horizon. This brief text added to the parable is directed to Christians to remind them that, just as the Jews remained outside the wedding banquet because of their attitudes, so too Christians can be excluded because of behavior that is not in keeping with the wedding feast and is unworthy of the call received.

It is interesting that in this passage the king (God) calls the guests through his servants. Without the work of these humble people, there would be no invitation to the banquet, and perhaps there would not even be a banquet, because in every royal palace, a banquet is prepared by the servants and not by the king. Those who have to lead the unworthy person out of the banquet hall and cast him into darkness (evil) are not simply household servants but personal servants of the king himself, namely, deacons. The reasons the guests do not come to the wedding are perfectly valid from the human point of view, but they are not valid to God. He first invites certain favored people, but they do not realize the importance of the invitation, and instead of immediately and joyfully accepting what is offered to them, they refuse, preferring their daily lives and mundane affairs, like planting a field. Some do not stop at rejecting the invitation but even insult the servants and kill them. The king then sends his troops to destroy the city and sends out his servants to invite whomever they can find and bring them to the wedding.

The parable is very clear. The king is God, who initially made a covenant with Israel. Although they were tenderly and passionately loved by God, this people refused to change their ways. When Israel was called to the wedding celebration—the most important of all love relationships—they did not participate because there were fields to sow, business to take care of, and all the things that normally people in love put aside when they know they are going to meet the love of their lives. These people prove themselves unworthy of his love.

God then turns to those considered unclean and unworthy of salvation, namely, everyone else, the non-Jews. However, even in this group, someone is not wearing appropriate clothes and has not acted as he should have to be admitted to the feast.

Those who will accept the invitation to the banquet become part of the Church, the new and everlasting Israel. This People of God is "new" because it is composed of people who belong not to the same ethnic group but to the community of faith; it is an "everlasting" People of God because it is also now an heir to the promises made to Israel, promises that cannot ever be broken because God made them. Unfortunately, both good and bad people come to the wedding, even people who are inappropriately dressed for an event of this kind, so another judgment is in order, and people will be punished for being unsuitably dressed. It is not enough to be called to the wedding feast; it is also necessary to demonstrate worthiness for that invitation.

THE PARABLE OF THE SOWER

Lk 8:4–8, 11–15

When a large crowd gathered, with people from one town after another journeying to him, he spoke in a parable. "A sower went out to sow his seed. And as he sowed, some seed fell on the path and was trampled, and the birds of the sky ate it up. Some seed fell on rocky ground, and when it grew, it withered for lack of moisture. Some seed fell among thorns, and the thorns grew with it and choked it. And some seed fell on good soil, and when it grew, it produced fruit a hundredfold." After saying this, he called out, "Whoever has ears to hear ought to hear." . . .

"This is the meaning of the parable. The seed is the word of God. Those on the path are the ones who have heard, but the devil comes and takes away the word from their hearts that they may not believe and be saved. Those on rocky ground are the ones who, when they hear, receive the word with joy, but they have no root; they believe only for a time and fall away in time of trial. As for the seed that fell among thorns, they are the ones who have heard, but as they go along, they are choked by the anxieties and riches and pleasures of life, and they fail to produce mature fruit. But as for the seed that fell on rich soil, they are the ones who, when they have heard the word, embrace it with a generous and good heart, and bear fruit through perseverance."

The Protagonists

The PROTAGONIST of this parable is the SOWER OF THE SEED, and we can identify him as Jesus. Although the sower is very aware that the seed is precious, he scatters it on all kinds of soil because he does not want any land deprived of it. Other sowers of the seed, with Jesus as a model, are all the people who dedicate themselves to spiritual teaching.

- Another protagonist on the same level as Jesus is the WORD OF GOD, which is the true agent that germinates the Kingdom of God in people's hearts.
- Like different soils, people's hearts are in different conditions in terms of being able to receive the Word of God.

For Reflection Together

- The sower has to carry an abundance of seeds; otherwise, the Kingdom of God can neither be planted nor increase. The sowers are those who fully accept carrying out the mission Jesus has entrusted to all Christians. Are you a sower of seeds?
- The Word of God is what needs to be sown. People can be tempted at times to sow their own words instead of the Word of God. What do you think about that? Can you give an example of the difference between the Word of God and the words of human beings?
- The seed falls on many different types of soil, just as there are many different types of people. What kind of soil do you think you are? Why? What kind of soil should you and would you like to be?

This parable refers to an experience that everyone in Israel might have had, namely, planting seed. The parable does not deal with large plots of land on the Galilean plain but with small fields on hillsides full of thorn bushes and brambles that are still seen near Capernaum, the city where Jesus lived for a while and where Peter's house is located. At one time, seeds were very scarce. To get them, farmers needed to give up part of the harvest from the previous year or to buy them, and no good farmer would have ever wasted any seed. However, even with careful planting, it was impossible for all the seed to end up in good soil because the texture of the soil could be poor.

Your
INTERACTION
with the
Text

We have two other versions of this parable (see Mt 13:1–9; Mk 4:1–9). The descriptive details of the agricultural terrain in all versions line up with the real situation at that time. Luke simplifies the story. His reference to the Word of God is clear (v. 11), and the Word becomes a protagonist in this parable. The one who comes to oppose the Word of God is the Devil (v. 12), who carries it out of the hearts of those who had accepted it. In these verses, Luke describes everyday life with the difficulties that Christians can encounter when they accept the Gospel and put into practice all that this entails. The parable likewise speaks of the work that needs to be done concerning the Word of God and its practical and fruitful actualization.

Rereading the Text Together

At the beginning of his work, the farmer does not know how things will turn out, but he continues to plant seed and wait for it to germinate and grow.

In a similar way, willing people can have the seed of the Word of God inside themselves that builds up the Kingdom of God as it ripens and matures. This happens above all through people's acceptance of God's love, which is then reciprocated by a desire to do his will in freedom and righteousness.

But in order for the Word of God to develop, the soil needs to be fruitful. It is people's responsibility to "plow" their own hearts little by little and remove the inner rocks, weeds, and other obstacles. It is not enough for the sower to scatter seed; it is necessary to do so in suitable soil. If the seed does not fall on fertile ground, it might still begin to germinate, but eventually the plant will dry up.

THE PARABLE OF THE MUSTARD SEED

Lk 13:18–19

Then he said, "What is the kingdom of God like? To what can I compare it? It is like a mustard seed that a person took and planted in the garden. When it was fully grown, it became a large bush and 'the birds of the sky dwelt in its branches.'"

Rereading the Text Together

The Kingdom of God is compared to a tiny mustard seed, one of the smallest seeds known at that time. It looks like a speck of dust. Whoever tries to evaluate the greatness of a tree by looking at the seed from which it grows will be making a serious mistake. The mustard seed, despite its smallness, contains a powerful force inside it that makes it grow into a tree that can accommodate the nests of various birds. The Kingdom of God is like a mustard seed. It too is very small at the beginning, too small to even talk about; its presence is nearly unnoticeable. However, when it takes root and becomes very strong and robust, it expands to the point of bringing its beneficial influence to every creature.

For Deeper Reflection

The image of the seed is especially dear to Jesus, because it clearly expresses the mystery of the Kingdom of God. In today's two parables it represents growth and contrast: the growth that occurs thanks to an innate dynamism within the seed itself and the contrast that exists between the minuscule size of the seed and the greatness of what it produces.

The message is clear: even though the Kingdom of God demands our collaboration, it is first and foremost a gift of the Lord, a grace that precedes man and his works. If our own small strength, apparently powerless in the face of the world's problems, is inserted in that of God it fears no obstacles because the Lord's victory is guaranteed. It is the miracle of the love of God who causes every seed of good that is scattered on the ground to germinate. And the experience of this miracle of love makes us optimists, in spite of the difficulty, suffering and evil that we encounter. The seed sprouts and grows because God's love makes it grow. May the Virgin Mary, who, like good soil, accepted the seed of the divine Word, strengthen within us this faith and this hope.

Pope Benedict XVI, *Angelus*
St. Peter's Square, June 17, 2012

The Signs of the Kingdom

THE RAISING OF THE YOUNG MAN IN NAIN

Lk 7:11–17

Soon afterward he journeyed to a city called Nain, and his disciples and a large crowd accompanied him. As he drew near to the gate of the city, a man who had died was being carried out, the only son of his mother, and she was a widow. A large crowd from the city was with her. When the Lord saw her, he was moved with pity for her and said to her, "Do not weep." He stepped forward and touched the coffin; at this the bearers halted, and he said, "Young man, I tell you, arise!" The dead man sat up and began to speak, and Jesus gave him to his mother. Fear seized them all, and they glorified God, exclaiming, "A great prophet has arisen in our midst," and "God has visited his people." This report about him spread through the whole of Judea and in all the surrounding region.

For this Jewish woman, the miracle is not an outside intervention by God that goes contrary to natural laws and modifies them. It is the ongoing creation on God's part that happens because God loves his people. There is a *dynamis*, a power, in Jesus. The actions he performs do not come simply from human power because it is actually God who is acting. It is the very glory and power of God that resides in the Temple in Jerusalem that is dwelling in Jesus.

People have always had fear, and fear of death in particular, and have attributed to God the power to give life and to take it away. Jesus' power is expressed in a specific way through the resurrection of the dead. When Jesus raises people from the dead, it foreshadows what will happen to him and what will happen to all human beings in the Kingdom of God. Jesus will be the first to experience a complete resurrection: Jesus is now alive forever, while those he raised from the dead later died.

Some men in the Bible are described as being men of God. Among them we can list Elijah, Elisha, Moses, Joshua, Daniel, and Joseph. However, none of them is the originator of what he does, and each is recognized as an intermediary between his action and God, who is the One truly responsible for the action.

Elijah raised the son of the widow of Zarephath from the dead (see 1 Kgs 17:17–24). However, when Elijah acted, he was using God's power. Jesus is the only one who demonstrates an ability to act by means of his own power and authority. Elisha also raised a young boy from the dead (see 2 Kgs 4:18–37). In both cases, the resurrection was of an only son and, in Elijah's case, the only son of a poor widow. Luke's intention here is to show that Jesus is also a great prophet. In addition, the episode furnishes details for the answer that will be given to John the Baptist, who asks if Jesus is the Messiah: the dead are raised, and this was an expected sign of the messianic age.

The small town of Nain is not far from the place in which Elisha performed his miracle, and it is also in the neighborhood of Nazareth.

In verse 13, Jesus is referred to as *Kyrios*, a title that was the name of God, YHWH, in the Greek translation of the Old Testament. Jesus is presented by Luke as a real man who can feel compassion, but at the same time, he is also truly God because he is able to intervene and give life back to someone who was dead and in the process of being buried.

The miracle, as Luke describes it to us, intends to reveal Jesus as the God who acts for the salvation of human beings and, in this case, who acts on behalf of a poor widow.

In raising this young man from the dead, Jesus is presenting himself as the Messiah and as God, the Lord of life, who is able to conquer death. This will become even clearer when he himself is raised.

There is, however, an important difference between the raising of the dead by Jesus and his own Resurrection. Those he raised from the dead would die again later, whereas Jesus' Resurrection is definitive because he is no longer dead. Jesus also shows himself to be the Merciful One who is able to be moved by the sorrow of the widow who has lost her only son.

Faith and miracles are inextricably tied together:

- People need to have faith to see God's intervention in history. Those who do not have faith cannot see the miracle and uselessly seek a sign their whole lives in order to believe. Believers, on the other hand, already know that God can act in their lives and thus interpret what happens through a particular lens. Along this line, for example, the people of Israel interpreted everything through the lens of the Exodus experience. Believers, however, are not limited to seeing God's action only in miracles but may also see it in the smallest occurrences in their lives.

- Believers and nonbelievers can experience similar circumstances. However, believers find God's hand in those circumstances, while those who do not believe do not benefit from seeing God's action because they deny it and are not in relationship with God.

- Faith is necessary for miracles. The people of Israel always had a hard time trusting God, but whoever had full confidence in YHWH never had to complain about any lack of assistance from God. People without faith can neither receive nor ask for a miracle because demanding one is a way of tempting God. An example of this occurred with the Israelites in the desert. They did not trust God's love, so they complained and tempted him to give them what they needed.

- A miracle, nevertheless, can be an ambiguous sign and not always easy to interpret, while words, which are also a means God uses to reveal himself, can be clearer. Words and miracles overlap, however, because words perform the task of interpreting the miracle.

- The interpretation of a sign, though, should take into account what the Church recognizes as consistent with faith. If an explanation is given to a sign that leads the hearer to choose apostasy (a denial of faith) instead of faith, that kind of explanation should not be accepted.

THE CALMING OF THE STORM AT SEA

Lk 8:22–25

One day he got into a boat with his disciples and said to them, "Let us cross to the other side of the lake." So they set sail, and while they were sailing he fell asleep. A squall blew over the lake, and they were taking in water and were in danger. They came and woke him saying, "Master, master, we are perishing!" He awakened, rebuked the wind and the waves, and they subsided and there was a calm. Then he asked them, "Where is your faith?" But they were filled with awe and amazed and said to one another, "Who then is this, who commands even the winds and the sea, and they obey him?"

The CONTEXT of the Passage

The Jews believed that God was the Lord of the universe, so as the Creator of all the forces of nature, he was the only one who could rule over them.

The Jews also had an experience of how dangerous water could be, especially the waters of the Lake of Galilee, which could drown people during a storm.

Your INTERACTION with the Text

Just as God's creation in Genesis, chapter 1, occurs by means of words, so too Jesus is able to control the elements of nature by his words.

The text does not say where this miracle occurred or whose boat was involved. According to Mark 4:39 and the following verses, the disciples despair because of what is happening and begin to cry out, but in Luke, their agitation is transformed into a desperate prayer to Jesus.

Jesus is sleeping (see Mt 8:23–27). The disciples are seized by fear and amazement but are incapable of interpreting the situation as a manifestation of God's power. Instead, they are perplexed and ask themselves who Jesus is.

Rereading the Text Together

Jesus acts in a way that leads the disciples to believe he is God. He actually has the power to "scold" the elements and calm them, demonstrating that he has power over nature's forces because he created them.

In addition, Jesus demonstrates that people can trust him because he is able to overcome the negative forces that try to prevail against human beings. Jesus knows he is the true salvation for all people, and people who have faith in him should never think that they are alone or that Jesus has "fallen asleep" and cannot help. Jesus is always present and acts according to the needs of all human beings and according to the needs of each individual, as if he or she were the only one he is taking care of.

THE MULTIPLICATION OF LOAVES

Lk 9:10–17

When the apostles returned, they explained to him what they had done. He took them and withdrew in private to a town called Bethsaida. The crowds, meanwhile, learned of this and followed him. He received them and spoke to them about the kingdom of God, and he healed those who needed to be cured. As the day was drawing to a close, the Twelve approached him and said, "Dismiss the crowd so that they can go to the surrounding villages and farms and find lodging and provisions; for we are in a deserted place here." He said to them, "Give them some food yourselves." They replied, "Five loaves and two fish are all we have, unless we ourselves go and buy food for all these people." Now the men there numbered about five thousand. Then he said to his disciples, "Have them sit down in groups of [about] fifty." They did so and made them all sit down. Then taking the five loaves and the two fish, and looking up to heaven, he said the blessing over them, broke them, and gave them to the disciples to set before the crowd. They all ate and were satisfied. And when the leftover fragments were picked up, they filled twelve wicker baskets.

For Reflection Together

- All the authors of the Gospels recount the miracles of Jesus for a reason that is quite different from curiosity about the spectacular, which is something that can appeal to all of us. Their goal is to demonstrate that Jesus is the Son of God. People are often tempted today to believe in magic or in odd supernatural occurrences. What do you think about that?
- What Jesus does during his public ministry is a sign of what will be completely manifested in his Paschal victory over death, and thus over the worst of evils, the evil that encompasses all the others. Do you believe in his victory?
- We cannot receive miracles from Jesus without faith. Faith in Jesus reaches its height of maturity in faith about his Resurrection—which becomes the great divide between those who believe in Jesus and those who do not. Do you believe in it?

The Israelites experienced being hungry when they were in the desert.

God responded to their physical hunger by sending manna, which nourished the people and kept them from starvation.

Manna, however, could not be kept for long, and those who tried to stock up on it discovered that it decomposed quickly. They did not have complete confidence in God and tried to take care of things themselves, through human means.

This event occurs after the disciples return from their first mission. The text shows the Twelve participating in Jesus' miracle to some extent. They do not understand what Jesus wants to do. He does not want the crowd to be sent away, but he does not want the disciples to go buy the necessary provisions either. The instruction that Jesus gives about organizing people in groups of fifty reflects the influence of Exodus, chapter 18. In the episode recounted there, Jethro, Moses' father-in-law, advised him to appoint judges so that he could be relieved of some of the work. Moses made the judges responsible for groups of people subdivided into various sizes, among which was a grouping of fifty (see Ex 18:21). The way the people were subdivided in that Exodus episode offers a clear structure for organizing this particular crowd, and Luke wants to recall that background from Exodus. His text also recalls another parallel with Exodus: the multiplication of loaves is reminiscent of the manna sent by God (see Ex 16:13–16).

The connection between the event of the multiplication of loaves and the Eucharist is very clear:

- Jesus tells the disciples to give the people food, which the Apostles will do by giving the Body of Christ to satisfy the spiritual hunger of the people who will believe.
- Jesus blesses and breaks the bread just as he will do at the Last Supper and in the Emmaus episode.
- Twelve baskets of bread are collected afterward, one for every tribe of Israel. This signifies the abundance and richness of the mission of the Church, the new Israel, which is accessible to all human beings.

Those who ate the manna quieted their hunger pains, but they were not satisfied. Jesus personally intervenes to feed the crowd, but he makes it clear that it is the Twelve who need to act and take care of the five thousand people. That is a considerable number of people and most probably intends to foreshadow the multitude of those who will believe the Gospel and will be taken care of by the Apostles.

In this episode, Jesus multiplies bread and fish, but he does so only after he tells the Twelve that it is their job to meet the needs of all those people. Being close to the needs of the people who hear the Gospel is, on some level, a continuation of the mission that they thought they had just finished.

However, the disciples do not know what to do. The provisions that Jesus and the Twelve have at their disposal are meager, and what is to be divided is not the least bit adequate for all the people. Those who participate in Jesus' miracles, even if only as spectators, recognize God's intervention if they have faith. Others, however, who do not believe in Jesus, can even maintain that the salvific actions of Jesus depend on the Devil (see Mt 12:22–30), or they take for granted that God is not involved in those actions (see Jn 9:16). Others are never satisfied by the signs Jesus gives and always demand other signs (see Mt 12:38–40, 16:4; Mk 8:11–12; Lk 11:14–16; Jn 6:30).

Jesus has difficulty performing miracles when he knows that the person asking for them does not have faith in him but wants to tempt him and put him to the test. Jesus does not want to be treated as a freak phenomenon and even less as a healer who needs to show off his power. The miracles Jesus performs are meant to be demonstrations that bring revelation and support his words—in addition to bringing freedom to the people who want to follow Jesus.

Jesus accompanies his words with many "mighty works and wonders and signs" (Acts 2:22), which manifest that the kingdom is present in him and attest that he was the promised Messiah.

The signs worked by Jesus attest that the Father has sent him. They invite belief in him. To those who turn to him in faith, he grants what they ask. So miracles strengthen faith in the One who does his Father's works; they bear witness that he is the Son of God. But his miracles can also be occasions for "offense" (Mt 11:6); they are not intended to satisfy people's curiosity or desire for magic. Despite his evident miracles, some people reject Jesus; he is even accused of acting by the power of demons.

Catechism of the Catholic Church, nos. 547–548

Indeed after Jesus, when he was about thirty years old, had left Nazareth and had already been traveling about preaching and working miracles of healing elsewhere, he once returned to his birthplace and started teaching in the synagogue. His fellow citizens "were astonished" by his wisdom, and knowing him as "the son of Mary," as the carpenter who had lived in their midst, instead of welcoming him with faith were shocked and took offense (cf. Mk 6:2–3). This reaction is understandable because familiarity at the human level makes it difficult to go beyond this in order to be open to the divine dimension. That this son of a carpenter was the Son of God was hard for them to believe. Jesus actually takes as an example the experience of the prophets of Israel, who in their own homeland were an object of contempt, and identifies himself with them. Due to this spiritual closure Jesus "could do no mighty work there [Nazareth], except that he laid his hands upon a few sick people and healed them" (Mk 6:5). In fact Christ's miracles are not a display of power but signs of the love of God that is brought into being wherever it encounters reciprocated human faith. Origen writes: "as in the case of material things there exists in some things a natural attraction toward some other thing, as in the magnet for iron, . . . so there is an attraction in such faith toward the divine power" (*Commentary on the Gospel of Matthew*, 10, 19).

Pope Benedict XVI, *Angelus*
Castel Gandolfo, July 8, 2012

Individual Encounters
with Jesus

THE RICH YOUNG MAN

Lk 18:18–30

An official asked him this question, "Good teacher, what must I do to inherit eternal life?" Jesus answered him, "Why do you call me good? No one is good but God alone. You know the commandments, 'You shall not commit adultery; you shall not kill; you shall not steal; you shall not bear false witness; honor your father and your mother.'" And he replied, "All of these I have observed from my youth." When Jesus heard this he said to him, "There is still one thing left for you: sell all that you have and distribute it to the poor, and you will have a treasure in heaven. Then come, follow me." But when he heard this he became quite sad, for he was very rich.

Jesus looked at him [now sad] and said, "How hard it is for those who have wealth to enter the kingdom of God! For it is easier for a camel to pass through the eye of a needle than for a rich person to enter the kingdom of God." Those who heard this said, "Then who can be saved?" And he said, "What is impossible for human beings is possible for God." Then Peter said, "We have given up our possessions and followed you." He said to them, "Amen, I say to you, there is no one who has given up house or wife or brothers or parents or children for the sake of the kingdom of God who will not receive [back] an overabundant return in this present age and eternal life in the age to come."

The
CONTEXT
of the
Passage

In this passage, Jesus is acknowledged as a wise Master, as some-one who can give advice to help people live fulfilled lives. Jesus maintained it was necessary to perform all the Law to be able to receive the fullness of life in God. To the Jews, living in fullness, being saved, however, meant above all being rich and not suffer-ing lack of any kind. The signs of a person's legal righteousness were his personal riches and his physical well-being and that of his family. However, God would credit a righteous man up to the fourth generation, so people could be unjustly rich if they possessed goods just because God was still rewarding their ancestors; these descendants could even be unworthy. In the context of this structured and complex manner of thinking about divine rewards, the Jews rarely took into account that the rich and powerful were often those who transgressed the Law more than the poor who were forced to expe-rience hunger and thirst. This raises the question about divine justice.

Throughout his Gospel, Luke always links wealth and power to something that is in conflict with God's justice. The rich and powerful person is always the one who does not completely observe the Law. In addition, Luke highlights the fact that wealth does not bring happiness but is instead a source of sadness. By contrast, those who are poor for the Kingdom of God are joyful (vv. 28–29).

The man asking Jesus the question here is a leader, someone who has a certain amount of power in Jewish society at that time. He calls Jesus "good teacher," and Jesus reminds him that only God is good and is the greatest source and expression of goodness. Jesus thus affirms that his own goodness can be understood as a reflection of the goodness of God that is revealed to everyone. Jesus calls this man to observe the Commandments, but he varies the order of the Commandments and ends with the one about honoring one's parents.

The young man asserts that he has always done all these things. Then Jesus asks him to renounce all that he has and give it to the poor. The young man is saddened because he is very rich. But his sadness also comes from the fact that he considers himself already perfect because he has always observed the Law. Jesus' teaching even seems too simplistic to him. Perhaps he was expecting to be given an ascetic discipline to follow. Jesus surprises him instead by asking him to let go of the external sign by which his countrymen would consider him as righteous: his riches. The riches on earth that Jesus asks him to renounce would have become treasures in heaven for him. In Luke, Jesus affirms that obtaining salvation is hard for a rich man. This concept is conveyed by the proverb about the difficulty of a camel passing through the eye of a needle. The crowd, however, does not understand. They are accustomed to thinking the rich are saved, and now Jesus has completely upset the apple cart. Peter remarks that they, the disciples, have followed him, and Jesus says that whoever has followed him has obtained much more already on earth and will obtain even more in heaven.

Rereading the Text Together

We have here a man who wants to be perfect and even believes that he is, but he cannot be perfect, because he is unable to live without his riches. What is interesting in Jesus' words is that it is not enough for him to sell everything and divest himself of goods, but he must give the proceeds to the poor. The new condition created by Jesus here requires that all those who intend to reach perfection must give a final sign of their intention and take one more step: share their goods. However, even this is not enough. After having given to the poor, he must also follow Jesus. "Come, follow me," he says, addressing him directly and individually (v. 22). Once again, we see Jesus setting up a personal relationship with the person he meets. Jesus' words and his calling are never generic; they are always personal, even though they are addressed to all human beings. Jesus never thinks of people as part of a generalized group; he always relates to the individual. It is true that Jesus calls *everyone*, but he calls *each person*.

The Protagonists

JESUS IS THE MAIN PROTAGONIST. He begins his teaching with the Old Testament but very quickly expresses the new requirement for whoever wants to be perfect. In a few sentences, he accomplishes a total reversal of the Jewish mindset of his day.

THE RICH YOUNG MAN. We do not know his age or anything about his appearance. We know that he is an important person who was very sure of himself and trusted in God very little. We also know that he is not open to giving away more than the Law required for almsgiving. He is someone who moves in a regressive direction: at the beginning, he seems to want to grow in perfection, but he pulls back when he understands what Jesus is asking of him.

THE LISTENERS are not identified. Nevertheless, they state the opinion of their day that only the rich are saved. They do not understand. Peter immediately remarks that the disciples can be saved because they have followed Jesus.

For Reflection Together

- Everyone has often heard that money does not bring happiness, but it is also true that money can be the source of trouble, suffering, and anxiety. Nevertheless, money is necessary for daily life. Jesus asks the rich young man to share his goods with the poor. What do you think about that?
- There is a good kind of wealth and a bad kind. What is the difference?
- Jesus' advice to the young man is limited to the distribution of his goods to the poor, but does Jesus' call involve something more than just his goods?
- What do you think it means for you at your age to follow Jesus? What riches do you possess that you are called to share?
- What should the young man have done to follow Jesus? What should you do?

ZACCHAEUS

Lk 19:1–10

He came to Jericho and intended to pass through the town. Now a man there named Zacchaeus, who was a chief tax collector and also a wealthy man, was seeking to see who Jesus was; but he could not see him because of the crowd, for he was short in stature. So he ran ahead and climbed a sycamore tree in order to see Jesus, who was about to pass that way. When he reached the place, Jesus looked up and said to him, "Zacchaeus, come down quickly, for today I must stay at your house." And he came down quickly and received him with joy. When they all saw this, they began to grumble, saying, "He has gone to stay at the house of a sinner." But Zacchaeus stood there and said to the Lord, "Behold, half of my possessions, Lord, I shall give to the poor, and if I have extorted anything from anyone I shall repay it four times over." And Jesus said to him, "Today salvation has come to this house because this man too is a descendant of Abraham. For the Son of Man has come to seek and to save what was lost."

The CONTEXT of the Passage

Jericho was a prosperous city in an important oasis right at the heart of the desert of Judea. Sycamores, which were found in that region, can grow very tall. We can still see sycamores there today and eat their fruit. Zacchaeus is a rich man who is spiritually far from Jesus. Zacchaeus functions as a contrast to the rich young man in Luke 18:18–30 and is an example of how a rich person can be saved.

Jesus goes to Jericho one day. Zacchaeus, the most important of the city's publicans, is so curious about Jesus that he wants at least to see him. However, there is a big crowd, and Zacchaeus is short, so he climbs a tree to see Jesus.

Jesus goes further than merely being seen by Zacchaeus. When he sees Zacchaeus's genuine interest, he takes the initiative and invites himself for a meal in his home.

Jesus' action provokes an immediate scandal for the inhabitants of Jericho who know Zacchaeus and consider him unclean because of his profession. They think that Jesus is being very cavalier and careless because he could have gone to eat with much worthier people who would have been very happy to host him.

A careful reading brings out certain facts:

- Jesus knows the publican's name before Zacchaeus speaks to him. (Jesus knows every person so intimately that he calls him or her by name.) Luke notes it was a large crowd, but despite all the commotion, Jesus is aware of this little man who climbed up a tree to see him. Jesus thus has full knowledge of all the people he deals with.
- Jesus brings salvation to the person who agrees to meet with him.
- When Jesus meets people, especially the poor and sinners, he wants to proclaim the Kingdom of God to them, and he does so in ways contrary to the conventions of the time.
- Jesus takes the initiative to convert people, help them, and bring them salvation.

Rereading the Text Together

Jesus invites himself to Zacchaeus's house not only to eat but also to lead his host to conversion. Zacchaeus developed an interest in Jesus, but his encounter with Jesus becomes decisive for him since he is transformed through it.

The Protagonists

JESUS IS THE MAIN PROTAGONIST because he takes the initiative to meet with Zacchaeus, a man who is very willing to meet with Jesus but would have been satisfied to see him from a distance. Jesus is always the one who takes the lead.

ZACCHAEUS is the chief publican, a rich man who is despised by all the citizens. We know nothing about his appearance except that he is so short that he is forced to climb up a sycamore because of the crowd. He is someone who goes through a rapid change. He is interested in Jesus, he acts immediately to be able to see him, he accepts him into his home, and he repents. We see only the result of this reformation: he restores fourfold to those he had defrauded and gives half of his goods to the poor.

THE TOWNSPEOPLE. All that we know about them is that they murmured against Jesus because he went to a publican's home to eat. Publicans' homes were unclean, so no observant Jew would have accepted having a meal in one of those homes for fear of contamination.

For a Jew to have a personal relationship with this kind of person was considered wrong.

No one understood why Jesus preferred to go to Zacchaeus's home and turn his back on the welcome of the city's respectable families.

For Deeper Reflection

Zacchaeus is small, and wants to see the Lord pass, and so he climbs a sycamore. Augustine says: "*Et vidit Dominus ipsum Zacchaeum. Visus est, et vidit.*" "And the Lord looked at Zacchaeus himself. Zacchaeus was seen, and therefore saw." What strikes one are those three seeings: that of Zacchaeus, that of Jesus, and then that of Zacchaeus again, after being seen by the Lord. "He would have seen Him pass even if Jesus had not raised his eyes, . . . but it would not have been a meeting. He would perhaps have satisfied that minimum of good curiosity out of which he had climbed the tree, but it would not have been a meeting" (p. 281). There is the point: some believe that faith and salvation come with our effort to look for, to seek the Lord. Whereas it's the opposite: you are saved when the Lord looks for you, when He looks at you and you let yourself be looked at and sought for. The Lord will look for you first. And when you find Him, you understand that He was waiting there looking at you, He was expecting you from beforehand. That is salvation: He loves you *beforehand*. And you let yourself be loved.

Cardinal Jorge Bergoglio, "Introduction,"
Giacomo Tantardini, *Il Tempo della Chiesa
Secondo Agostino*, 2009

Jesus blesses Zacchaeus for his pledge: "If I have defrauded anyone of anything, I restore it fourfold" (Lk 19:8). Those who, directly or indirectly, have taken possession of the goods of another, are obliged to make restitution of them, or to return the equivalent in kind or in money, if the goods have disappeared, as well as the profit or advantages their owner would have legitimately obtained from them.

Catechism of the Catholic Church, no. 2412

The Beatitudes

When he saw the crowds, he went up the mountain, and after he had sat down, his disciples came to him. He began to teach them, saying:

"Blessed are the poor in spirit,
    for theirs is the kingdom of heaven.
Blessed are they who mourn,
    for they will be comforted.
Blessed are the meek,
    for they will inherit the land.
Blessed are they who hunger and thirst for righteousness,
    for they will be satisfied.
Blessed are the merciful,
    for they will be shown mercy.
Blessed are the clean of heart,
    for they will see God.
Blessed are the peacemakers,
    for they will be called children of God.
Blessed are they who are persecuted for the sake of righteousness,
    for theirs is the kingdom of heaven.

Blessed are you when they insult you and persecute you and utter every kind of evil against you [falsely] because of me. Rejoice and be glad, for your reward will be great in heaven. Thus they persecuted the prophets who were before you."

The Mount of Beatitudes

The Mount of Beatitudes is located about 492 feet above the Lake of Galilee. There is a convent of Franciscan sisters on the summit of this small hill that overlooks the lake and provides a very beautiful panorama. The lovely Church of the Beatitudes, built by the architect Antonio Barluzzi in 1937, rises up from an octagonal base, a design that reflects the number of Beatitudes in Matthew. The mosaic floor inside depicts symbols for the seven virtues: the three Theological Virtues (faith, hope, and charity) and the four Cardinal Virtues (justice, prudence, fortitude, and temperance). The church is very simple and is surrounded by a portico from which the Lake and the Plain of Galilee can be seen. Everything here is immersed in silence. The location is very evocative, helping people to recall Jesus' words and inviting them to meditation. The Lucan tradition sets the delivery of this sermon a bit lower at Tabgha, almost on the shores of the lake. From the point of view of faith, it is not important to discover the precise location of the delivery of this sermon. We do know, however, that the locations around this lake were the ones most frequented by Jesus, who lived there for a number of years.

God had given Israel the Law so that they could always be united to him in an eternal covenant. For this reason, the Jews believed that the Torah, the first five books of the Bible (Genesis, Exodus, Leviticus, Numbers, and Deuteronomy), was similar to the Ketubah, a document that seals a marriage contract. God acts like a king who promulgates his laws. Moses is the mediator of this holy covenant. The Decalogue is composed in the style of an ancient treaty between a powerful sovereign and the kings who paid him tribute. This kind of treaty included laws that the sovereign established for the people under his rule. God reveals himself as the true King of his people, the One who, like a king who is well aware of his royal function, intends to protect and guide his people, procuring every blessing and the salvation promised to them. He requires, however, the people's commitment, their faithfulness, and their respect of the Law.

Although the Law is contained in the first five books of the Bible, people often cite only the Ten Commandments of the Mosaic covenant, which contains the principal guidelines not only for an Israelite but for every human being. This Law, according to tradition, was given to Moses by God on Mount Sinai.

Christians also have a kind of code with very specific laws, the Sermon on the Mount, which contains a synthesis of Jesus' teaching.

For Christians, the Gospel consists in preaching about the risen Christ, who, precisely because he is risen, gives people a guarantee that his teaching is not simply the teaching of a learned master but is the very Word of God. Just as God wanted to give his people instruction through the laws of the covenant so that they would live in a way that is holy, so too Jesus taught people to do good to others and to understand God's plan's in depth. He taught them how to become holier because the Lord is holy.

For Reflection Together

- The message of the Beatitudes is stirring but at the same time demanding. Each Beatitude corresponds to a human need (a need for mercy, for peace, etc.) that people try to respond to as best they can. The message functions as a guide about what people should devote themselves to in order to meet Jesus' expectations on some level.
- According to what you know, in what areas has the Church tried to involve itself as a response to the model of the Beatitudes? Identify at least three areas in which the actions of the Church seem very important in terms of following one of the Beatitudes recommended by Jesus.
- Why do you think the message of the Beatitudes is considered to be especially powerful for young people in every age and nation?

Just as the Law is contained in five books, so too the Sermon on the Mount in Matthew's Gospel constitutes what is said to be the preeminent teaching among Jesus' five great teachings (the other four being the missionary discourse, the discourse on the Church, the eschatological discourse, and the parables). It involves material drawn from Jesus' teaching that occurred not during a single event but throughout his whole time of teaching, and Matthew collected it here in this form.

Luke also records the text of this new law (see Lk 6:20 ff.), but he does not include some sections that are in Matthew. The sections he omits would have been of major interest for Matthew's audience, a community that had many Jewish Christians, but would have been of little interest for Luke's audience, the Greeks. These two passages are referred to as the Sermon on the Mount (Matthew) and as the Sermon on the Plain (Luke). The authors of these two texts have chosen different settings to offer us a different set of parallels. Placing this sermon on a mountain means comparing it to the Decalogue received by Moses on Mount Sinai. Jesus would then be the new Moses, the new Legislator who receives the new law from God and transmits it for people to observe. He presents a law that completes that of Moses. In Matthew, Jesus is the Master who teaches with *exusia*, with power, but this power comes from God and not from human beings. It is his authority that makes new life possible for Christians.

Luke instead has Jesus speaking on a plain because he wants to recall a different event in Exodus. Moses came down from the mountain and read the Law to Israel right before they made a covenant with God. It is because of this Old Testament event that we find not only Beatitudes in Luke but also curses, "woes," since each section of the covenant in Exodus includes curses.

Matthew presents eight Beatitudes, while Luke records four Beatitudes and four woes. Matthew's goal is to offer a blueprint for life to those who intend to live virtuously based on Jesus' example. Luke wants to present a complete reversal of what people consider earthly blessings to be, because in the Kingdom of Heaven things will be inverted.

Formulas for blessedness are not unknown in the Old Testament and appear in Wisdom literature (see Ps 1:1–2, 33:12, 127:5–6; Prv 3:4; Sir 31:8) and in documents discovered in Qumran. However, the happiness promised in the Old Testament was something earthly, whereas Jesus places the fulfillment of blessedness in the Kingdom of Heaven and in messianic salvation.

There is a clear eschatological tension in this sermon, both in Matthew and Luke.

The two versions establish a kind of identity card for a Christian and set out fundamental principles for conduct and for choices that should characterize Christian life. Although no action or behavior is prohibited in the Beatitudes, Jesus offers the example of how a Christian should behave.

Matthew starts the list of Beatitudes in verse 3 with the statement that in order to enter the Kingdom of Heaven one must be poor (*ptokos*), one must be in need and ask for help. While Luke 6:20 refers to material poverty, in Matthew, it is poverty of spirit that is the issue, an attitude of the human heart. However, the poor in Luke belong not to a sociological category but to a theological one, since they are the recipients of the news of freedom, of the year of grace, and of forgiveness. God favors whoever is a victim of people's scorn or derision: the blind, the lame, the deaf, all those who would be set free at the time of the Messiah's manifestation. They are therefore blessed because God carries out that liberation here and now for people in those situations. The poor in Matthew have a certain similarity to the *anawe-ruah* of the Old Testament (see Ps 69:33; Prv 14:21; Is 29:19).

The promises in the Old Testament are aimed at the poor who sum up and represent the religious ideal. They are the ones who open their hearts to God in times of affliction and thirst for the good; they trust in God on every occasion, even during the sorrowful times in life. They are meek, merciful, and simple. They work for peace and benefit from God's promises and the messianic blessings.

The ideal described here is represented in a perfect way by Jesus.

The land referred to in verse 5 is the land promised to Israel by God. However, that land becomes spiritualized and is now the heavenly homeland.

Verse 6 speaks of hungering and thirsting for righteousness. In the Old Testament, God promised the Israelites he would meet all their needs. However, the people were supposed to practice righteousness by being faithful to God and his Law. For Jesus, the hunger and thirst here are no longer physical needs but spiritual ones that lead us to the quest for moral perfection. As people seek moral perfection, God on his part will ensure the spiritual blessings needed to attain it.

Verse 7 recalls that mercy in the Old Testament is an attribute of God, who reveals himself as "a God gracious and merciful" (Ex 34:6). Here the reference is instead to the Christian law of forgiveness: forgive in order to be forgiven.

Verse 8 speaks about "the clean of heart." In the Old Testament, cleanliness, especially ritual cleanliness, was a very serious issue. Jews could not eat all foods or perform actions that would expose them to uncleanness, and if they did, they were obliged to undergo a ritual of purification that could be very complicated. The text here emphasizes inner purity. It is in fact from the heart, from a person's inner being, that all evil comes forth. On this point, Jesus' teaching is connected to that of the Prophets (see Is 1:10–17; Hos 6:6; Am 4:1–5). At one time, Jews thought it was impossible to see God because his holiness was so powerful it would crush a human being: whoever sees God dies! Only the elders of Israel, immediately after accepting the covenant in Exodus, were able to take part in a banquet in God's presence and yet live. Seeing God means being able to enjoy his grace and his presence. However, only people who are "clean of hand and pure of heart" (Ps 24:4) can enjoy this intimacy.

Verse 9 deals with peace. In the Bible, the Hebrew word *shalom* means not merely the absence of strife but a state in which a person or a people live in total fullness of life. This state of blessedness would occur at the time of the coming of the Messiah. In the Old Testament, we often see people involved in war as they conquered the Promised Land and defended themselves from attacks by foreign nations. However, peace in the Bible is never separated from justice (see Ps 85:11). Working for peace fundamentally means being co-workers with God.

Verse 10 tells of persecution for those who labor for the Kingdom of Heaven. Contrary to the thinking of his time, Jesus does not consider persecution a reason to seek divine vengeance against persecutors but considers it a situation for experiencing blessedness and entering the Kingdom of Heaven.

Rereading the Text Together

Matthew's Gospel presents Jesus as the Teacher of the New Covenant. At the heart of Jesus' teaching, his Gospel, is the proclamation of Beatitudes that completely overturns our idea of happiness.

According to Jesus, the poor, the suffering, the persecuted, and those who labor for peace are the blessed ones. We tend to think that rich, powerful, and successful people are the happy ones! The poor that Jesus speaks about are all those who think that happiness cannot be bought with money and that more important things lead to happiness. Jesus teaches us to look at reality from God's point of view and his plan of love.

Blessed are the ones who choose to accept God's plan, act according to God's will, and trust completely in him. They do not think of themselves as "rich" in anything (even if they have many goods). They know that they owe everything to the Father's love and that everything they possess is a gift from God. They know that their good qualities can be used in service on behalf of other people, justice, peace, and truth.

The rich, whom the world considers truly "blessed," do not belong to the group of the blessed according to Jesus' teaching. Material wealth, if people have it, needs to be thought of as a great responsibility and as something to be used to serve and benefit the whole community. For this reason, whoever has many goods has the duty to share them with those in need.

▶

The people who follow Jesus accept the message of the Beatitudes and place themselves in service to their brothers and sisters. But who are the really blessed people? How do we recognize them? According to Matthew, the "blessed" are first of all the poor in spirit, the people who

- Recognize that everything they have, including life, comes from God. Even if they are rich in personal gifts (charisms) or in economic and social gifts, they realize those gifts never fully belong to them. They can use personal wealth for themselves and for others, but they need to administer it knowing it is not theirs.
- Accept having a mindset in line with God's thinking even when they do not fully understand. They are people who let themselves be guided by God and led on unknown paths.
- Do not think that material goods are the most important things in life. People need to steward those goods because everything is a gift from God. However, the most important gifts are certainly not constituted by wealth.
- Are not violent and do not try to get the better of their neighbor.
- Fight for justice and peace and are willing to go against the current. They do not get involved with the powerful, the overbearing, and the violent because they will never accept playing those games. They do not take part in persecution.
- Are not afraid of life or of getting their hands dirty, even knowing that doing so could mean the loss of all material goods and even of life. They act this way because it is just and humane.
- Have decided for the course of their lives to conform themselves to a model and have chosen Christ. They have not stopped thinking for themselves, but they recognize that Jesus' words lead to life.
- Oppose sin and evil and do not walk on the path of vengeance. They are capable of genuine love and genuine forgiveness.

For Deeper Reflection

The Beatitudes depict the countenance of Jesus Christ and portray his charity. They express the vocation of the faithful associated with the glory of his Passion and Resurrection; they shed light on the actions and attitudes characteristic of the Christian life; they are the paradoxical promises that sustain hope in the midst of tribulations; they proclaim the blessings and rewards already secured, however dimly, for Christ's disciples; they have begun in the lives of the Virgin Mary and all the saints.

Catechism of the Catholic Church, no. 1717

Let us remember the Prophet Isaiah who says that even if our sins were scarlet, God's love would make them white as snow. This mercy is beautiful! I remember, when I had only just become a bishop in the year 1992, the statue of Our Lady of Fatima had just arrived in Buenos Aires and a big Mass was celebrated for the sick. I went to hear confessions at that Mass. And almost at the end of the Mass I stood up, because I had to go and administer a First Confirmation. And an elderly woman approached me, humble, very humble, and over eighty years old. I looked at her, and I said, "Grandmother"—because in our country that is how we address the elderly—"do you want to make your confession?" "Yes," she said to me. "But if you have not sinned. . . ." And she said to me: "We all have sins. . . ." "But perhaps the Lord does not forgive them." "The Lord forgives all things," she said to me with conviction. "But how do you know, Madam?" "If the Lord did not forgive everything, the world would not exist." I felt an urge to ask her: "Tell me, Madam, did you study at the Gregorian [University]?", because that is the wisdom which the Holy Spirit gives: inner wisdom focused on God's mercy. Let us not forget this word: God never ever tires of forgiving us! "Well, Father what is the problem?" Well, the problem is that we ourselves tire, we do not

want to ask, we grow weary of asking for forgiveness. He never tires of forgiving, but at times we get tired of asking for forgiveness.

Let us never tire, let us never tire! He is the loving Father who always pardons, who has that heart of mercy for us all. And let us too learn to be merciful to everyone. Let us invoke the intercession of Our Lady who held in her arms the Mercy of God made man.

Pope Francis, *Angelus*
St. Peter's Square
March 17, 2013

The Lord's Prayer

Mt 6:7–15

"In praying, do not babble like the pagans, who think that they will be heard because of their many words. Do not be like them. Your Father knows what you need before you ask him.

This is how you are to pray:
Our Father in heaven,
    hallowed be your name,
    your kingdom come,
    your will be done,
        on earth as in heaven.
    Give us today our daily bread;
    and forgive us our debts,
        as we forgive our debtors;
    and do not subject us to the final test,
        but deliver us from the evil one.

If you forgive others their transgressions, your heavenly Father will forgive you. But if you do not forgive others, neither will your Father forgive your transgressions."

For the Jews who thought they were permanently in God's presence and should therefore always be holy, religious practice was very important. The Jews thought that every event in a person's life depended on God, who always knows what a person needs and provides it. Joys and sorrows, poverty and riches, health and sickness, life and death—everything depended on God.

The Jews of Jesus' time did not gather at the Temple for prayer because they considered that sanctuary to be God's house, so it was the place to worship him and offer sacrifices. Prayers were said at home (personal and family prayer) or in a synagogue (community prayer) three times a day: morning, noon, and evening. Usually they recited the *Shema Israel* (the central Jewish prayer for morning and evening drawn primarily from Deuteronomy 6:4–9), or they prayed the Psalms, the great prayers of Israel that the Church inherited.

Jesus taught the Apostles to pray, but they marveled when they often saw him pray because his prayer was silent and internal. In ancient times, people were accustomed to praying out loud so that they could be heard by God. However, the prayers of Christians should not be like the prayers of pagans who multiply their words; they should be like the trusting and simple conversations people have with their fathers.

We have two versions of the Lord's Prayer, this one from Matthew and a shorter one from Luke. It is difficult to know which one is Jesus' original prayer. It is important to note, however, that tradition decided to keep both versions. According to the *Didache*, a document at the end of the first century AD, the early Christians used to recite the Our Father three times a day.

The text of the prayer comes out of a Jewish environment and reflects the influence of Old Testament texts reread by Jesus, who revitalizes them with a new spirit.

The prayer presents seven requests. (The number seven is a symbol of human perfection and is favored by Matthew, who often uses it in his Gospel.) The first three requests concern the Reign of God and his coming, while the other four deal with needs in every person's life. Some scholars have related the Our Father to Jesus' prayer in the Garden of Olives (see Mt 26:39–42).

The word "Father" in verse 9 translates the word *Abba*, which actually means "Daddy." It is usually the name small children use for their fathers until they are older. This is the special and unique way that Jesus addressed God, expressing his filial confidence toward God because he was his Son. The Jews for the most part simply used the word *Ab*, which means "Father," and avoided addressing God as "my Father." Believers, following Jesus' example and his explicit invitation, began to address God in this very intimate way.

This is a Father who is "in heaven," explicitly indicating that he is not an earthly father. For Israel, God is the Holy One par excellence, and holiness was one of his special attributes. To draw near to the holiness of God, people needed to be in a certain state of purity. The name of the Lord should not be profaned. In the Bible, it is God who sanctifies his name (see Ez 36:23), making known his wisdom, goodness, and justice—each of these being one of his divine attributes. The prayer, then, asks God to show his holiness specifically through the coming of his Kingdom, a request that is also part of the Kiddush, a Jewish prayer for blessing the Sabbath.

The Kingdom that is asked for is the promised and awaited one. It represents the complete fulfillment of the messianic age. His Kingdom, however, cannot fully come to pass if people do not agree to do God's will. Doing God's will is in fact how his Kingdom comes. Only Christ is able to do God's will perfectly.

The request for earthly needs to be met is limited to today's needs, so it concerns people's immediate needs. The text shows the influence of the Old Testament passage in which God sends manna in the desert so the Israelites could be nourished, but the manna did not last for more than a day at a time (see Ex 16:4, 19–20). The daily bread here is similar to the daily rations that were given to the fighting men. In the first century, the people were waiting for a messiah who would bring an abundance of material blessings, but Jesus reminds us that material goods should be strictly the necessary ones.

Sin, an offense to God, is likened to a debt we owe that remains insolvent. People's debt cannot be remitted if they have not, at the time of their prayer, already forgiven their own debtors.

The text also speaks of asking God for help in times of temptation so that people do not succumb to doing evil.

Rereading the Text Together

Jesus does not hide when he prays but allows himself to be seen by his disciples and teaches them to love prayer, which should be a joy rather than a duty. Prayer is a vital part of life for Jesus. The disciples are struck by the way Jesus prays and ask him to teach them to pray. Jesus then composes the very beautiful Our Father.

The innovative element of this prayer is that, in addressing God, people consider him as a Father rather than as a master. Everything good that is given to God's children comes from him. Because people recognize God as the unique source of good, they address their requests to him for the things they need. People who use the words Jesus taught know that the greatest good is doing the Father's will, so they pray to him for assistance in doing it. People who do the Father's will know they have to forgive offenses because God the Father will apply the same measure of mercy to people that they use in dealing with others. The Lord's Prayer is actually a great model that all Christians can use to formulate their own personal prayer, and it can be used for meditation and renewal.

Jesus is presented in Luke's Gospel as a man who prays often (see Lk 3:21, 5:16, 6:12, 11:1–4, 22:41–42). Jesus' prayers are very special because they are a kind of loving conversation between the Son and the Father. Jesus' approach becomes a model of how to relate to God. During prayer, people can ask for help, to have strength and courage in life's difficulties, and can also praise and thank God for all that they have received.

For Deeper Reflection

"Our awareness of our status as slaves would make us sink into the ground and our earthly condition would dissolve into dust, if the authority of our Father himself and the Spirit of his Son had not impelled us to this cry . . . 'Abba, Father!'. . . . When would a mortal dare call God 'Father,' if man's innermost being were not animated by power from on high?" (St. Peter Chrysologus, *Sermon* 71, 3)

This power of the Spirit who introduces us to the Lord's Prayer is expressed in the liturgies of East and of West by the beautiful, characteristically Christian expression: *parrhesia*, straightforward simplicity, filial trust, joyous assurance, humble boldness, the certainty of being loved.

Catechism of the Catholic Church, nos. 2777–2778

For Reflection Together

- Jesus does not pray because he has to but because he wants to; he desires to pray and considers it important. What is your attitude toward prayer?
- The Lord's Prayer is a special way of approaching God. He is not a severe master and father but a real Father from whom a person receives all that is good in life. How do you address God in prayer?
- People need to actively, and not passively, accept what God has planned for them in doing his will because God cannot ever choose evil for human beings, the very creatures he loves more than all other creatures. It is Jesus himself who offers the example of how people should live. However, doing God's will can be difficult and also costly for people. What do you think it means in your life to do God's will?
- Doing the Father's will includes forgiving offenses because the same measure with which we have forgiven others is the measure with which we will be forgiven. How do you approach forgiving offenses from others?
- True evil, the most dangerous evil, dwells in the heart of every person; it is the personal self-centeredness that everyone needs to deal with. How does self-centeredness manifest itself in your life?
- Being freed from evil means knowing it is possible to overcome evil because there is a Person who has conquered it before us. After his Crucifixion, Christ overcame death, the symbol of the worst evil for human beings, once and for all. What does it mean in your life to believe that Christ has conquered evil and death?
  What are the results of believing this?
  What attitudes demonstrate a believer's faith in the freedom from evil and death that Christ brings us?

God, Rich in Mercy: The Merciful Father

Lk 15:11–32

"A man had two sons, and the younger son said to his father, 'Father, give me the share of your estate that should come to me.' So the father divided the property between them. After a few days, the younger son collected all his belongings and set off to a distant country where he squandered his inheritance on a life of dissipation. When he had freely spent everything, a severe famine struck that country, and he found himself in dire need. So he hired himself out to one of the local citizens who sent him to his farm to tend the swine. And he longed to eat his fill of the pods on which the swine fed, but nobody gave him any. Coming to his senses he thought, 'How many of my father's hired workers have more than enough food to eat, but here am I, dying from hunger. I shall get up and go to my father and I shall say to him, "Father, I have sinned against heaven and against you. I no longer deserve to be called your son; treat me as you would treat one of your hired workers."' So he got up and went back to his father. While he was still a long way off, his father caught sight of him, and was filled with compassion. He ran to his son, embraced him and kissed him. His son said to him, 'Father, I have sinned against heaven and against you; I no longer deserve to be called your son.' But his father ordered his servants, 'Quickly bring the finest robe and put it on him; put a ring on his finger and sandals on his feet. Take the fattened calf and slaughter it. Then let us celebrate with a feast, because this son of mine was dead, and has come to life again; he was lost, and has been found.' Then the celebration began. Now the older son had been out in the field and, on his way back, as he neared the house, he heard the sound of music and dancing. He called one of the servants and asked what this might mean. The servant said to him, 'Your brother has returned and your father has slaughtered the fattened calf because he has him back safe and sound.' He became angry, and when he refused to enter the house, his father came out and pleaded with him. He said to his father in reply, 'Look, all these years I served you and not once did I disobey your orders; yet you never gave me even a young goat to feast on with my friends. But when your son returns who swallowed up your property with prostitutes, for him you slaughter the fattened calf.' He said to him, 'My son, you are here with me always; everything I have is yours. But now we must celebrate and rejoice, because your brother was dead and has come to life again; he was lost and has been found.'"

The CONTEXT of the Passage

YHWH is a good God who watches over Israel, even if, like every father, he has to intervene in order to instruct his people about how to live.

The Protagonists

GOD THE FATHER IS THE MAIN PROTAGONIST. He rules the Kingdom of Heaven. He loves people so deeply that he leaves them free to make mistakes, but he has the patience to wait for them to return home and admit their wrongdoings.

THE YOUNGER SON who decides to leave home is the prototype of all sinners and therefore of all human beings.

THE ELDER SON is an example of a person who thinks he is in the right and boldly condemns others for their misconduct. He does not want his father to welcome his own brother home, just like many Christians today who prefer that sinners would simply be condemned and not forgiven. Even some people who have not physically distanced themselves from the Father have distanced themselves mentally and spiritually because they fail to love. Those people are thus not free of sin themselves and are in the same situation as the older brother.

This episode in Luke's Gospel tells the story of a rich man who has two sons who will inherit his wealth. The outward behavior of the two sons is different because one serves the father faithfully, and the other decides to leave at a certain point and asks the father for his part of the inheritance.

The father would be within his rights not to give his son anything because, since he is still alive, his son cannot legally ask for anything. The father leaves his son free and respects his will because he knows that holding him back by force would only be detrimental. The son receives his inheritance and travels far away. This young man, however, is very immature and squanders what he has until he reduces himself to misery and further degrades himself by being a pig herder. (Pigs were unclean animals to the Jews.) Only when he hits bottom does the irresponsible young man recognize his bad behavior and repent of the choices he made. He realizes that being in his father's house is a better way to live, even it means being taken back as a servant, because the servants there are at least treated with dignity. Meanwhile, the father all this time has not forgotten his son and has been waiting for his return. As soon as the son speaks, the father, aware of his repentance, welcomes him home.

The story also includes a second son, who always remained faithful and who is jealous of his brother because the father has restored the younger son's status and arranges a feast for him.

For Reflection Together

- All human beings find themselves in the situation of the son who left his father's house. People waste their inheritance and end up as pig-herders. In our own lives, these "pigs" are situations in which we contaminate ourselves spiritually. What do you think about that?
- Christians can run the risk of finding themselves in the older brother's situation. They believe they have the right to something more just because they behave well, and they want others who made mistakes to be forgotten, punished, and rejected, even when they repent. Can you think of an example of this?
- The overflowing love of the father in the parable is manifested when he does not hold back the son who wants to leave as well as when he forgives the son who is eaten up with envy. The Father waits for each person to understand his or her wrongdoing and repent. In the Sacrament of Penance, people can meet the Father who welcomes them at the door of his home. What do you think about this?

Rereading the Text Together

The parable points to the Father who does not give up loving people, even when they refuse his love. He is not in a hurry and knows how to wait for those who left him to understand, repent, and return so that he can then show them his love. In the Kingdom of Heaven, the return of a son or daughter is a reason to celebrate with great feasting. However, the parable also presents the example of someone who thinks he is in the right only because he has always been faithful and who is jealous now because his father also loves the younger brother who had wasted all his inheritance.

Jesus wants us to understand the following through this parable:

- God is a Father who loves all human beings without exception, and his love is not based on their behavior.
- God faithfully waits for people to understand they have done wrong.
- When people distance themselves from God, God never abandons them but waits for them at the door to celebrate with a feast.
- There are people, however, who refuse the Father's love.
- The Father is always ready to forgive.
- It is important to acknowledge the wrongdoing we have committed, to recognize ourselves as sinners, and to return to the Father like children.
- No one can maintain that he or she is in the right.
- All human beings are children of God, whom he loves with equal intensity.
- No one can judge another's conscience.
- Everyone should love God and do his will out of love and not out of duty.
- No one should be envious of the love God has for other people.

For Deeper Reflection

The process of conversion and repentance was described by Jesus in the parable of the prodigal son, the center of which is the merciful father: the fascination of illusory freedom, the abandonment of the father's house; the extreme misery in which the son finds himself after squandering his fortune; his deep humiliation at finding himself obliged to feed swine, and still worse, at wanting to feed on the husks the pigs ate; his reflection on all he has lost; his repentance and decision to declare himself guilty before his father; the journey back; the father's generous welcome; the father's joy—all these are characteristic of the process of conversion. The beautiful robe, the ring, and the festive banquet are symbols of that new life—pure, worthy, and joyful—of anyone who returns to God and to the bosom of his family, which is the Church. Only the heart of Christ who knows the depths of his Father's love could reveal to us the abyss of his mercy in so simple and beautiful a way.

Catechism of the Catholic Church, no. 1439

The Empty Tomb

On the first day of the week, Mary of Magdala came to the tomb early in the morning, while it was still dark, and saw the stone removed from the tomb. So she ran and went to Simon Peter and to the other disciple whom Jesus loved, and told them, "They have taken the Lord from the tomb, and we don't know where they put him." So Peter and the other disciple went out and came to the tomb. They both ran, but the other disciple ran faster than Peter and arrived at the tomb first; he bent down and saw the burial cloths there, but did not go in. When Simon Peter arrived after him, he went into the tomb and saw the burial cloths there, and the cloth that had covered his head, not with the burial cloths but rolled up in a separate place. Then the other disciple also went in, the one who had arrived at the tomb first, and he saw and believed. For they did not yet understand the scripture that he had to rise from the dead. Then the disciples returned home.

The Tomb

Jewish tombs were usually carved into a huge rock. Inside there was a vestibule with a stone table for preparing burial clothes and other materials and then a room for the actual burial. In the burial room, niches were carved into the walls where the dead bodies were laid. The tomb's low entrance, which was sometimes decorated, was closed off by a large round stone that was rolled along a track to make the sepulcher airtight so that animals could not get in. It was impossible to move the rock from inside because it was so large and heavy. Only several people on the outside could roll it away.

According to the Gospel, Jesus of Nazareth was crucified toward the sixth hour (noon) and died around the ninth hour (3:00 p.m.). Jesus was given the most severe treatment for criminals. However, his legs were not broken because when the Roman guard came to see if Jesus had died yet, he thrust his sword only into Jesus' side, the so-called "death blow" with which the death of a condemned man was officially verified.

The bodies of those condemned to death were legally the property of the state. Since they were considered unclean by the Jews and could not be buried with other dead people, their bodies were thrown into a common grave. Jesus' body, however, did not undergo this fate because Joseph of Arimathea, a noble member of the Sanhedrin who had recently had a new sepulcher built for his family, asked for the body of Jesus so he could bury him.

Jewish sepulchers of well-to-do families in Jerusalem were carved out of a rock and had more than one room. Behind the small opening, the vestibule had a stone table, where final preparations were carried out for the burial. The Jews generally did not mummify dead bodies. According to Jewish custom, bodies would be first washed and then carefully shaved. Then they were washed again and anointed with perfumed oils. Finally, the body would be wrapped in a shroud. The body was then placed in the innermost room, where niches were carved into the wall.

According to the synoptic Gospels, there was not enough time to complete the burial of Jesus that had begun in haste because it was the Friday evening before the

Sabbath. The Sabbath was a day in which no one could perform a burial without violating the law about Sabbath rest and without becoming contaminated.

According to John's account, the women prepared the spices, intending to finish the burial on the morning after the Sabbath. John's Gospel says that Nicodemus bought one hundred pounds of strong perfumes (bags of aloe and myrrh) and put them around the body of Jesus, probably to preserve the body. The women who were preparing Jesus' burial knew very well the location in which their Master was buried, as opposed to what the detractors of the Christians later said.

On Sunday, the first day of the week, which would become the Lord's Day for Christians, Mary of Magdala, also known as Mary Magdalene, arrives at the tomb. The synoptic Gospels refer to several women, but John mentions only Mary Magdalene. However, he does so in a way that includes the others because Mary speaks in the plural: "We don't know where they put him."

The women probably come to the tomb to finish the burial. According to John 19:40–42, they could not finish the burial preparation for Jesus' body because that was the day of preparation for the Passover. If they had completed the burial process, their contact with a dead body would have made them unclean and therefore unable to take part in the prescribed rituals for the Jewish Passover.

Luke and John recount that Peter went to see what happened to Jesus' body. John records that the disciple "whom Jesus loved" reaches the tomb first; perhaps because he was younger than Peter, he "ran faster." Arriving at the tomb, the disciple whom Jesus loved leans in and sees the burial cloths in the same spot they were in before, but he does not enter first. Meanwhile, Peter arrives and realizes that the burial cloth that wrapped Jesus body is right where it had been left, but Jesus' body is no longer inside it. According to eyewitness testimony, the burial cloths had been removed from the body but were not left crumpled on the floor, as they would have been if thieves had taken the body. It seemed instead that Jesus' body had "vanished" and that the burial clothes were put back exactly where they had been. The cloth that had been wound around Jesus' head—probably to avoid having the mouth open up and remain open at burial—was rolled up in a separate place. The details of the grave cloths probably convinced John that something extraordinary had happened. If his body had been stolen, things would not have been left in this condition.

It is important to notice the verbs "to see" and "to believe" here—"he saw and believed" (Jn 20:8)—a key theme that appears throughout John's Gospel. These verbs are linked to the important theme of "sign." In John's Gospel, Jesus performs extraordinary signs like the raising of Lazarus (see Jn 11:1–44). However, these signs are not interpreted in the same way, and people's various interpretations reveal their inner orientations. In the case of Lazarus, some people believe, while others not only do not have faith but also want to attack Jesus. The fate of Jesus is in fact decisively determined immediately after Lazarus' resurrection (Jn 11:45–54). The chief priests and the Pharisees said, "'What are we going to do? This man is performing many signs.' . . . So from that day on they planned to kill him" (Jn 11:47, 53). The two verbs "see" and "believe" establish a context in which "believe" refers to something supernatural. This does not concern seeing and believing as something that happens on a purely earthly and physical level but as something beyond that. Those who do not believe, according to John, belong to the darkness, and the darkness did not receive him: "The world did not know him. . . . His own people did not accept him" (Jn 1:10–11). However, to those who believed, "he gave power to become children of God, to those who believe in his name, who were born not of natural generation nor by human choice nor by a man's decision but of God" (Jn 1:12–13).

Rereading the Text Together

The discovery of the empty tomb that the author of the fourth Gospel presents is constructed with quite sophisticated narrative techniques.

Mary Magdalene, even though she is a woman, is the first to become aware that something odd has happened at the tomb, something that nobody expected. She goes to the disciples to tell them Jesus' body has disappeared. John tells us what Mary Magdalene says but not what Peter and "the disciple whom Jesus loved" say in response. These two disciples, who had shared some important experiences, take off running after they hear what she has to say to verify what really happened. Peter, who is older, needs a longer time to get there, while the younger disciple, who is vigorous and very eager to discover what is going on, arrives and looks inside while cautiously standing outside to wait for his older companion. When Peter arrives, they go inside and face a strange situation. The burial clothes wrapped around Jesus' body have been put back right where they had originally been. Nothing seems to have been touched, and the shape of Jesus' body can still be seen imprinted on the burial cloth that the women's skillful and loving hands had wrapped around his arms and legs.

Because of what they see, they finally understand things that Jesus had told them before. However, the key they use to interpret this event is the *Scriptures*. Facing the sign of the empty tomb and armed with the key to interpretation that had been entrusted to all of Israel, they are able figure out what happened. They immediately understand, in retrospect, what had been written, and now they recognize that the *Scriptures* spoke about Jesus and his Passion, Death, and Resurrection.

For Deeper Reflection

"Why do you seek the living among the dead? He is not here, but has risen" (Lk 24:5–6). The first element we encounter in the framework of the Easter events is the empty tomb. In itself it is not a direct proof of Resurrection; the absence of Christ's body from the tomb could be explained otherwise. Nonetheless the empty tomb was still an essential sign for all. Its discovery by the disciples was the first step toward recognizing the very fact of the Resurrection. This was the case, first with the holy women, and then with Peter. The disciple "whom Jesus loved" affirmed that when he entered the empty tomb and discovered "the linen cloths lying there," "he saw and believed" (Jn 20:2, 6, 8). This suggests that he realized from the empty tomb's condition that the absence of Jesus' body could not have been of human doing and that Jesus had not simply returned to earthly life as had been the case with Lazarus.

Catechism of the Catholic Church, no. 640

— — — — — — — — — — — — — — — —

Christ's Resurrection was not a return to earthly life, as was the case with the raisings from the dead that he had performed before Easter: Jairus' daughter, the young man of Naim, Lazarus. These actions were miraculous events, but the persons miraculously raised returned by Jesus' power to ordinary earthly life. At some particular moment they would die again. Christ's Resurrection is essentially different. In his risen body he passes from the state of death to another life beyond time and space. At Jesus' Resurrection his body is filled with the power of the Holy Spirit: he shares the divine life in his glorious state, so that St. Paul can say that Christ is "the man of heaven."

Catechism of the Catholic Church, no. 646

— — — — — — — — — — — — — — — —

In the *Creed* we repeat these words: "and rose again on the third day in accordance with the Scriptures." This is the very event that we are celebrating: the Resurrection of Jesus, the center of the Christian message which has echoed from the beginning and was passed on so that it would come down to us. St. Paul wrote to the Christians of Corinth: "I delivered to you as of first importance what I also received, that Christ died for our sins in accordance with the scriptures, that he was buried, that he was raised on the third day in accordance with the scriptures and that he appeared to Cephas, then to the Twelve" (1 Cor 15:3–5). This brief profession of faith proclaims the Paschal Mystery itself with the first appearances of the Risen One to Peter and the Twelve: *the death and Resurrection of Jesus are the very heart of our hope.*

Without this faith in the death and Resurrection of Jesus our hope would be weak; but it would not even be hope; or precisely the death and Resurrection of Jesus are the heart of our hope. The Apostle said: "If Christ has not been raised, your faith is futile and you are still in your sins" (v. 17). Unfortunately, efforts have often been made to blur faith in the Resurrection of Jesus and doubts have crept in, even among believers. It is a little like that "rosewater" faith, as we say; it is not a strong faith. And this is due to superficiality and sometimes to indifference, busy as we are with a thousand things considered more important than faith, or because we have a view of life that is solely horizontal. However, it is the Resurrection itself that opens us to greater hope, for it opens our life and the life of the world to the eternal future of God, to full happiness, to the certainty that evil, sin and death may be overcome. And this leads to living daily situations with greater trust, to facing them with courage and determination. Christ's Resurrection illuminates these everyday situations with a new light. The Resurrection of Christ is our strength!

Pope Francis, General Audience
St. Peter's Square, April 3, 2013

For Reflection Together

- We have read one of the most important passages of the New Testament, which is known as "Running to the Tomb." We have tried to reconstruct what could have happened and what the two Apostles might have seen. The author of the fourth Gospel tells us in fact that he saw and believed, so it is important for us to know exactly what he saw. Try to construct what happened yourself.
- However, an empty tomb in itself is not a guarantee of Jesus' Resurrection because, like all signs, it can be ambiguous. How do the two disciples know what happened, and what makes them interpret it in a way that leads them to believe in the Resurrection of Jesus?
- Can an empty tomb affect the faith of a group of people so much that they are led to leave their former lives behind and dedicate themselves to evangelization? Their understanding of the event is tied to a rereading of some Old Testament Scriptures and their reinterpretation. Even today, faith comes forth from a bold **proclamation** and a **new reading** of the heritage of faith, which the Church is called to witness to and the faithful are called to receive. In your experience, how are these two things tied together?
- The discovery of Jesus' empty tomb raises the urgent question of who Jesus is. How do you answer this question, which is so fundamental to faith?

Mary Magdalene: The First Herald of the Gospel

Jn 20:1–2, 11–18

On the first day of the week, Mary of Magdala came to the tomb early in the morning, while it was still dark, and saw the stone removed from the tomb. So she ran and went to Simon Peter and to the other disciple whom Jesus loved, and told them, "They have taken the Lord from the tomb, and we don't know where they put him.". . .

But Mary stayed outside the tomb weeping. And as she wept, she bent over into the tomb and saw two angels in white sitting there, one at the head and one at the feet where the body of Jesus had been. And they said to her, "Woman, why are you weeping?" She said to them, "They have taken my Lord, and I don't know where they laid him." When she had said this, she turned around and saw Jesus there, but did not know it was Jesus. Jesus said to her, "Woman, why are you weeping? Whom are you looking for?" She thought it was the gardener and said to him, "Sir, if you carried him away, tell me where you laid him, and I will take him." Jesus said to her, "Mary!" She turned and said to him in Hebrew, "Rabbouni," which means Teacher. Jesus said to her, "Stop holding on to me, for I have not yet ascended to the Father. But go to my brothers and tell them, 'I am going to my Father and your Father, to my God and your God.'" Mary went and announced to the disciples, "I have seen the Lord," and what he told her.

The Protagonists

MARY MAGDALENE is a woman who appears twice in John's Gospel, first at the Cross (see Jn 19:25) and again in John 20:1–18. She is an important person who is clearly portrayed, even if John does not describe her appearance or her age. This indefiniteness is perhaps meant to help the reader identify with her. She is someone who believed in Jesus but felt abandoned when he died. When she discovers the body is missing, she is dejected, but she immediately recognizes the Lord when he calls to her.

JESUS is hard to recognize now because his appearance has changed so much after his Resurrection. He is unrecognizable even by someone like Mary Magdalene, who loved him so dearly. Jesus can now be recognized only through his words. Jesus personally calls her and entrusts her with the important task of bringing the Good News to his disciples.

Israelite culture considered women to be inferior to men. They were under the charge of a father, a husband, or a brother, and widows generally had very difficult lives. A rabbi could not speak to a woman who was not a family member, and a woman's testimony at trial was given exactly half the value of a man's. Entrusting any message to a woman was therefore considered a bad idea.

Luke presents women who have special relationships with God: Elizabeth, the mother of John the Baptist, and Mary, the Mother of God. They are both collaborators in salvation history.

Many women assist Jesus and his Apostles: Mary Magdalene, Joanna (the wife of Chuza), Susanna, and others. Jesus is not afraid to be close to the sinful women that he converts (see Lk 7:36–50).

Jesus' friends also include Martha and Mary, the sisters of Lazarus in Bethany (see Lk 10:38–42). The Gospel recounts that Mary was seated at Jesus' feet to hear him speak. This was considered very improper in Jewish culture. Jesus raises the daughter of Jairus from the dead (see Lk 8:41–42, 49–56). Women are the first ones to be aware that Jesus is no longer in the tomb and has been raised from the dead, and they are also the first ones to proclaim his Resurrection.

In John's Gospel, there are many women who play important roles: the Mother of Jesus (who is never referred to by name) (see Jn 2:1–12; 19:25–27); the Samaritan woman Jesus meets at the well (see Jn 4:1–42); the woman caught in adultery (see Jn 8:1–11); Martha and Mary (see Jn 11:1–6, 17–36); and finally, Mary Magdalene,

who performs a very significant role. John's Gospel presents Mary Magdalene, who had already been seen at the foot of the Cross, as the first person not only to discover the empty tomb but also to see the Risen One. In addition, she is entrusted with the first proclamation to the Apostles.

For Reflection Together

- Try to reread the text slowly.
- Try to put yourself in Mary Magdalene's shoes.
- What does it mean to her to have lost Jesus' body? Who took him away? Why is she crying?
- Whom does Jesus call by name at this point? What is the assignment that Jesus entrusts to everyone?

Your
INTERACTION
with the
Text

This passage recounts Mary's experience at Jesus' tomb on the first day of the week. The authors of the other Gospels mention a group of women who come to finish burying Jesus. Their presence is important for establishing the facts that follow. After their news about finding the tomb empty, they will be accused of being mistaken and of not going to the right tomb in which Jesus was buried. Is it very likely that the women did not know the burial location of the person in whom they had placed all their hopes?

The other Gospels report that the group of women arrives on Sunday morning, the first day of the week, with the spices and perfumed oil they had prepared in order to finish the burial process that had hurriedly begun on Friday. John, who stylistically prefers to present one person at a time, names only Mary Magdalene in this case, so that he can weave in her powerful dialogue with Jesus. John, however, is aware that there were several women at the tomb and has Mary use the plural when she says, "We don't know where they put him" (Jn 20:1). Mary then draws aside, away from the other women. The other women have come to Jesus' tomb to perform very specific functions, while Mary instead has come to the tomb without a clear purpose, or at least John does not reveal it to us. He already said that Nicodemus had brought an enormous quantity of aloe and myrrh for Jesus' burial—about one hundred pounds of it (see Jn 19:39–40)—so there was no need for him to list these ointments again here.

So why does Mary Magdalene go to the tomb? It is for a personal reason. Mary wants to see the person she loved one more time, the person who had died on the Cross and been taken away forever. Wanting to see him again, this disciple is in the right state to encounter the Risen One.

Mary Magdalene goes to the tomb and sees that the stone has been rolled away. The text does not say if she entered at this point, yet she runs to Simon Peter and the disciple Jesus loved and tells them, "They have taken the Lord from the tomb, and we don't know where they put him." Why did Mary Magdalene think that someone had stolen the body when she saw the open tomb? And what is the significance of her using the title "Lord" here that could point to his divinity? Mary is thinking about the possible theft of Jesus' body, so she is not yet able to recognize God's action in the very fact that the body is missing.

John's account is constructed to demonstrate the confusion Mary is experiencing: "It was still dark" (Jn 20:1), and the darkness makes it difficult to see anything clearly.

The text presents the two disciples running to the tomb together, and we can imagine that Mary is running back too, given that the following scene shows her outside the tomb crying. With Jesus' body missing, the last link she could have with the Master and the opportunity to mourn for him is gone.

It is at this point that Mary leans over into the tomb and sees two angels in the place where Jesus' body had been laid. When the angels ask her why she is crying, she says, "They have taken away my Lord" (Jn 20:13).

Very soon after, the same conversation is repeated, but this time, the one asking the question is Jesus, and Mary mistakes him for the gardener because she is preoccupied with finding Jesus' body.

In verse 9, John tells us that up to this point, before they "saw and believed," the Apostles had not understood the Scriptures and were not prepared for something like a resurrection. Mary expresses her desire for the return of Jesus' body three times, showing her complete lack of preparedness as well.

In verse 15, Jesus asks Mary, "Whom are you looking for?" rather than, "What are you looking for?" The body of a dead person, precisely because that person was loved, is always "someone" and not "something."

Only when Jesus calls her by her name—"Myriam" (Mary)—does she recognize him.

Jesus' Resurrection changed his body, and it is now transfigured. That fact is apparent in the episode of the two disciples going to Emmaus (see the text from Luke 24 on pages 76–77). Jesus was recognized by the signs he performed, but now Mary recognizes him only when she hears him call her. In the fourth Gospel, the reader is told earlier that "the sheep hear his voice, as he calls his own sheep by name and leads them out" (Jn 10:3).

With Jesus' call to her, we are no longer just listening to an extraordinary dialogue between the risen Jesus and a disciple; we are overhearing a very personal call, "Mary." Jesus knows this disciple and calls her by name, and Mary responds by calling him "Rabbouni," a title that acknowledges him as her Master. It is very probable that Mary had called Jesus "Master" dozens of times before, but her use of that title here is charged with drama as she recognizes that Jesus is indeed her Master.

This encounter is designed to be brief and to draw quickly to a close because Jesus can no longer be met in the flesh; he can no longer be recognized by physical eyes but only through proclamation and with the eyes of faith. Mary, who wanted so very much to find Jesus' body, is now called to believe in a different way and to forego an encounter on the natural level. She had met Jesus when he was alive in a physical body, she had wept at the foot of the Cross, she had known he was being buried, and now she is the first to believe in Jesus even though she will no longer be able to see him or touch him. Like all other believers in history, Mary needs to be willing to recognize Jesus through his words and is now called to be a witness to the faith this way, a witness even to the Apostles.

In fact, Jesus entrusts Mary with the task of proclaiming to the Apostles that he is risen. Mary Magdalene is thus the first herald of the Gospel of Jesus: "Go to my brothers and tell them, 'I am going to my Father and our Father, to my God and your God.'" When Mary goes to announce to them, "I have seen the Lord!" she uses a Greek word that translates the divine tetragrammaton (the four consonants YHWH that form the name of God revealed to Moses on Sinai). Mary's faith is now complete. Jesus is the Lord. Jesus is God.

Rereading the Text Together

It is mostly the apocryphal gospels that develop Mary Magdalene's personality. This episode offers a very dramatic scene that artists in every age have tried to represent in statues, icons, and literature. Popular tradition has developed the figure of Mary Magdalene wrongly now and then. The human situation of this woman, profoundly overcome with grief that might well change her life forever, is quite striking. Mary was a disciple of Jesus. At the foot of the Cross, we see only Jesus' Mother, his mother's sister, Mary Clopas, and Mary Magdalene. It is not important how she became Jesus' disciple, but her presence at the Cross makes her a perfect witness. Mary is attached to Jesus by a profound love. His loss devastates her, and she runs to and fro in an agitated state like a moth flitting around a lamp. But it was dark! Not entering the tomb, Mary finds herself in the darkness of terror and doubt: "They have taken the Lord." Three times, she expresses her desire to get the body back. She has a connection to this body: she wants it back so she can weep over it, grieve over it, perhaps for the rest of her life.

However, Jesus specifically calls her by name, "Mary," and is able to make her recognize him immediately the way sheep recognize the voice of their shepherd. It is helpful to note here that in the Old Testament, God is the Shepherd of Israel (see Gn 49:24; Ps 23, 80:2; Jer 31:10; Ez 34:11–22), and Israel is his flock. The Master and Shepherd that Mary Magdalene recognizes is not just the man Jesus, the authoritative Master she had met; he is also Lord and God.

Mary is called to believe even though she can no longer see the Lord she loved so much, even though she can no longer encounter him in his earlier physical appearance. She knows him now only through his word to her.

In addition, Mary is called to proclaim the Gospel and is the first to do so.

Jesus entrusts a woman with the *kerygma*, the first proclamation to his disciples.

Like Mary Magdalene, all those who love Jesus are called to believe in him through the word he addresses to them, and that word is a person's name, a personal calling, "Mary."

Those who are called are also invited to participate in the proclamation.

Mary Magdalene and the holy women who came to finish anointing the body of Jesus, which had been buried in haste because the Sabbath began on the evening of Good Friday, were the first to encounter the Risen One. Thus the women were the first messengers of Christ's Resurrection for the apostles themselves. They were the next to whom Jesus appears: first Peter, then the Twelve. Peter had been called to strengthen the faith of his brothers, and so sees the Risen One before them; it is on the basis of his testimony that the community exclaims: "The Lord has risen indeed, and has appeared to Simon!" (Lk 24:34).

Catechism of the Catholic Church, no. 641

After his appearances to the women, others follow. Jesus makes himself present in a new way, he is the Crucified One but his body is glorified; he did not return to earthly life but returned in a new condition. At first they do not recognize him and it is only through his words and gestures that their eyes are opened. The meeting with the Risen One transforms, it gives faith fresh strength and a steadfast foundation. For us too there are many signs through which the Risen One makes himself known: Sacred Scripture, the Eucharist, the other Sacraments, charity, all those acts of love which bring a ray of the Risen One. Let us permit ourselves to be illuminated by Christ's Resurrection, let him transform us with his power, so that through us too the signs of death may give way to signs of life in the world.

I see that there are large numbers of young people in the square. There you are! I say to you: carry this certainty ahead: the Lord is alive and walks beside you through life. This is your mission! Carry this hope onward. May you be anchored to this hope: this anchor which is in heaven; hold the rope firmly, be anchored and carry hope forward. You, witnesses of Jesus, pass on the witness that Jesus is alive and this will give us hope, it will give hope to this world, which has aged somewhat, because of wars, because of evil and because of sin. Press on, young people!

Pope Francis, General Audience
St. Peter's Square, April 3, 2013

Recognizing Jesus

Lk 24:13–35

Now that very day two of them were going to a village seven miles from Jerusalem called Emmaus, and they were conversing about all the things that had occurred. And it happened that while they were conversing and debating, Jesus himself drew near and walked with them, but their eyes were prevented from recognizing him. He asked them, "What are you discussing as you walk along?" They stopped, looking downcast. One of them, named Cleopas, said to him in reply, "Are you the only visitor to Jerusalem who does not know of the things that have taken place there in these days?" And he replied to them, "What sort of things?" They said to him, "The things that happened to Jesus the Nazarene, who was a prophet mighty in deed and word before God and all the people, how our chief priests and rulers both handed him over to a sentence of death and crucified him. But we were hoping that he would be the one to redeem Israel; and besides all this, it is now the third day since this took place. Some women from our group, however, have astounded us: they were at the tomb early in the morning and did not find his body; they came back and reported that they had indeed seen a vision of angels who announced that he was alive. Then some of those with us went to the tomb and found things just as the women had described, but him they did not see." And he said to them, "Oh, how foolish you are! How slow of heart to believe all that the prophets spoke! Was it not necessary that the Messiah should suffer these things and enter into his glory?" Then beginning with Moses and all the prophets, he interpreted to them what referred to him in all the scriptures. As they approached the village to which they were going, he gave the impression that he was going on farther. But they urged him, "Stay with us, for it is nearly evening and the day is almost over." So he went in to stay with them. And it happened that, while he was with them at table, he took bread, said the blessing, broke it, and gave it to them. With that their eyes were opened and they recognized him, but he vanished from their sight. Then they said to each other, "Were not our hearts

burning [within us] while he spoke to us on the way and opened the scriptures to us?" So they set out at once and returned to Jerusalem where they found gathered together the eleven and those with them who were saying, "The Lord has truly been raised and has appeared to Simon!" Then the two recounted what had taken place on the way and how he was made known to them in the breaking of the bread.

The city of Emmaus that the Gospel speaks about is a little more than seven miles from Jerusalem. Various small cities around Jerusalem today claim to be the Emmaus of the Gospel, but it has not been possible to pinpoint the city precisely. It is generally identified today either as El-Qubeibe or Abu Gosh, both of which are northwest of Jerusalem.

The Protagonists

THE TWO DISCIPLES on the road to Emmaus. We know that one was called Cleopas, but we know nothing about the other one. Their description is minimal, but this vagueness can function to help a reader walk alongside them. In this brief passage, the two disciples evolve from having a lack of faith to a fullness of faith that blossoms into proclamation. Cleopas has an intense conversation with Jesus that reflects what many believers would have liked to say. The conversation allows Jesus to reveal himself and offer a key for interpreting the facts.

JESUS IS THE MAIN PROTAGONIST, whose identity needs to be discovered. The two disciples do not succeed in discovering it because they do not recognize him. Their eyes are blinded, so they do not know who he is. As soon as they do recognize Jesus, he disappears.

Your
INTERACTION
with the
Text

Luke 24:13–35 deals with an event that appears only in his Gospel. It is still Sunday, the first day of the discovery of the empty tomb and of Jesus' Resurrection. Luke records that on that very day two disciples are walking to Emmaus. We do not know exactly who these two disciples were. We know that one is named Cleopas but nothing else. Earlier in verse 9, Luke speaks of the eleven, so these two are not Apostles; they probably belonged to the group of people mentioned in verse 33 who are said to be with the Apostles. Luke does not tell us what time of day this episode takes place. In addition, at the end of his account, he refers in verse 34 to an appearance of Jesus to Simon without saying anything specific about it. The two disciples are downcast as they are discussing what has been happening. The topic concerns the truly extraordinary events that had taken place. Jesus, in whom they had hoped so much, is dead, and his tomb has been found empty.

In verse 15, Luke identifies Jesus for the reader, but the two disciples have not yet experienced their fundamental transition to faith. Jesus approaches them, but the disciples mistake him for a man on a journey, a pilgrim. He is with them, but they do not really see him; they do not recognize him or know his name. The two disciples lack the keys to understand, they lack the Paschal light by which to interpret the Death and Resurrection of Jesus. The "pilgrim" asks them what they are talking about, so they tell him about Jesus of Nazareth and what happened to him. They are dejected and in crisis. One of them, Cleopas, tells him that they had hoped

Jesus was the Messiah. The two disciples had maintained high hopes of a Messiah. They trusted in Jesus when others had not believed his words, and their expectation was appropriate in a Jewish religious environment. In other words, they believed Jesus would show himself to be a powerful Messiah because of the signs he performed during his public life; they hoped he would liberate his people. However, no messiah for the Jews could ever die on a cross. Despite their hopes, death had put an end to the Nazarene affair. What happened to Jesus was nothing less than a tragedy to them.

Despite their thorough knowledge about Jesus and what had happened to him, they are not able to understand the salvific significance of the event.

In verses 18–35, the two disciples give a rather precise report of what had occurred. What they say closely parallels what is presented in Acts 2:22ff. However, the story of Jesus, a powerful man called the Nazarene, ends with his Death on the Cross. What follows this tragic event, in addition to their disappointment, is the very vague description of the testimony of the women and the experience of "some of those with us." The way the text describes the women's faith and the perplexity of the Apostles indicates that the two disciples are more inclined to align themselves with the Apostles who doubted the women's report.

The story from the women, instead of increasing their faith, is a reason for distress. The news about the empty tomb does not cause their faith to be stirred but instead leaves them dismayed. In itself, the news that Jesus' body was not in the tomb causes only perplexity, ambiguity, and bewilderment. The tomb is empty, so now what? The body could have been stolen or . . . .

In reality, faith cannot spring forth simply from knowing that Jesus' body is no longer where it had been placed after his Death. In order for faith to rise up, the proclamation of the Resurrection needs to happen, the very thing that the women heard from the angel that can be interpreted this way.

Jesus then interprets for the two disciples the prophecies about the Messiah and explains to them that the suffering and Death of the Christ are necessary and are the only ways the Nazarene could have entered into glory.

The disciples are close to Emmaus, and it is evening. They insist that the pilgrim stop and have dinner with them, which is one way that people in the East show kindness and hospitality. At table, Jesus breaks the bread, blesses it, and gives it to them according to the Jewish custom of having the guest bless the bread. Luke presents several occasions in which Jesus blesses the bread before distributing it. We find that kind of blessing in the multiplication of the loaves (see Lk 9:16); during the Last Supper with the Apostles (see Lk 22:19); and then here (Lk 24:30).

The account of the two disciples moves quickly to an echo of the Last Supper. It is interesting to note that Luke, when he tells of Jesus' appearances, links his being recognized to a very clear sign or to a word (see Lk 24:30–31), and we see this approach in John as well (see Jn 20:14, 16, 20). We have to remember that Jesus' body was transfigured after the Resurrection. The two disciples recognize him only in the gesture of blessing and breaking the bread, but as soon as they recognize him, he disappears. In Luke's Gospel, Jesus is "seen" the moment he disappears; he goes away even to the point of concealing himself in heaven (see Luke 24:51; Acts 1:9ff).

As soon as they recognize Jesus, they understand why their hearts were burning within them. Through his words, the light of truth in the Old Testament is combined with the light of inspired interpretation, and now it is possible for them to understand the facts and to recognize Jesus.

It is only at this point that the two disciples can make the fundamental crossover that every believer has to make, the step of moving from knowing everything about the man Jesus to believing that he is indeed the Christ, the Son of God, the Risen One, God-with-us.

Immediately, the two disciples understand that Jesus is truly risen, and as soon as they arrive in Jerusalem, they communicate that to the Apostles. There is now corroborating evidence from these two witnesses as well.

Rereading the Text Together

Everything takes place during a short journey along the dusty streets of Judea. The details of the trip are important to Luke, who formulates the writing of his Gospel and Acts as the great journey of the Word (Jesus) who comes from Nazareth to Jerusalem, where he is put to death, is raised, and shows himself to be alive to his followers. Nevertheless, the story of the Word does not end here. In Acts of the Apostles, the Word will be carried by the Apostles as far away as Rome, the center of the known world at that time. Luke is saying through this that the Word of God must reach all human beings. In future journeys there will be other groups of people who walk, who do not stop, who move forward, and who are on a great mission.

There are some significant elements to note in this passage:

- The sadness of the two disciples on their way to Emmaus
- Their profound knowledge about things concerning Jesus that they keep up-to-date
- The amazement of the two disciples, who almost mock the pilgrim because he seems so out of touch and ignorant about what has happened
- The initial incredulity of the two disciples in not believing the women and their solidarity with the Apostles who mistrust the news about the empty tomb
- The encounter with Jesus, whom the author and the reader recognize but who is unknown to the two disciples whose eyes are blinded
- The explanation from the Scriptures by Jesus, a method that will be used by the first community in its initial proclamation of faith
- The recognition of Jesus through his signs
- The ensuing disappearance of Jesus
- The sad hearts that are slow to understand, which become burning hearts when they learn that the facts about Jesus were already foreseen in the Scriptures
- The faith of the two disciples who bring the news to the Apostles

In this passage, Jesus

- Speaks, teaches, and reveals the Scriptures
- Sits at the table and breaks bread
- Appears and disappears

The body of the Risen One is present, alive, and truly in their midst. His glorified body is different from the bodies that people have during their lives on earth, but Jesus is clearly not just a disembodied soul.

The two disciples are prototypes of people who are well informed and know everything there is to know about Jesus, and yet they are still not believers. In fact, they have not been able to go from knowing Jesus as a man to believing that

▶

Jesus is the Son of God. It is a risk that all believers run. They think they know Jesus because they know what he has said and done. They know the environment in which he was born and lived, they are able to recount the facts about his last three days before his Death, but they do not really know him. They think he is simply a fellow traveler but certainly not God. Something is needed for this recognition to happen. The Word of God can be used as an interpretive key, and this is what Jesus does in interpreting the Scriptures for them.

At this point, their eyes are opened, and they are able to see, to know, to recognize this person in front of them as the Other whom they had never experienced this way. A sign marks their authentic encounter with divinity: their hearts burn within them. Luke's account does not end here but continues until the two disciples share their story with the eleven Apostles. They had shared the Apostles' doubt about believing the news from the women, but they are now united in faith with the eleven about Jesus' Resurrection. What has changed in the meantime is their ability to interpret events, so they can now acknowledge with the others that "the Lord has truly been raised and has appeared to Simon!" (Lk 24:34).

Although the climax of the passage occurs when they recognize Jesus in the breaking of the bread, Luke leads the reader to one more issue that is essential for a Christian, which is that of testifying. Whoever recognizes Jesus can do nothing less than proclaim him. We see this evolution of faith in the two disciples:

- From the beginning, they adhered to Jesus' preaching, believing he was a powerful prophet and perhaps even the Messiah that Israel was awaiting.
- Their hope is disappointed. The chief priests and civil authorities put him to death, and this decisive action shuts down their hopes.
- They cannot, therefore, believe that he was the Messiah they were expecting.
- Next, their hearts burn as they hear Jesus instructing them about how to interpret the story of Israel, his own story, and their story.
- They recognize Jesus from the signs of blessing and breaking the bread.
- As soon as they reach Jerusalem, they tell the disciples everything that happened to them during the time they were with Jesus.

The two disciples go from not being believers to proclaiming Jesus. They have completed a great spiritual journey in knowing who Jesus really is.

For Reflection Together

- What was the disciples' state of mind?
- Why are they in this state?
- Why do they not recognize Jesus?
- What does Jesus do?
- What makes the disciples realize that they are talking and eating with Jesus?
- What is the action that Jesus performs linked to?
- What do the disciples do next?
- Is Jesus acknowledged today as the Son of God?
- Who is Jesus to you? Is he an important figure, a friend, a revolutionary, a man of the people, a prophet, a messiah, a philosopher, the Son of God? Why?
- What do the two disciples do when they go back to Jerusalem?

For Deeper Reflection

The Scriptures had foretold this divine plan of salvation through the putting to death of "the righteous one, my Servant" (Is 53:11) as a mystery of universal redemption, that is, as the ransom that would free men from the slavery of sin. Citing a confession of faith that he himself had "received," St. Paul professes that "Christ died for our sins in accordance with the scriptures" (1 Cor 15:3). In particular Jesus' redemptive death fulfills Isaiah's prophecy of the suffering Servant. Indeed Jesus himself explained the meaning of his life and death in the light of God's suffering Servant. After his Resurrection he gave this interpretation of the Scriptures to the disciples at Emmaus, and then to the apostles.

Catechism of the Catholic Church, no. 601

John's Gospel tells us that Jesus appeared twice to the Apostles enclosed in the Upper Room: the first time on the evening of the Resurrection itself and on that occasion Thomas, who said unless I see and touch I will not believe, was absent. The second time, eight days later, Thomas was there as well. And Jesus said, speaking directly to him, I invite you to look at my wounds, to touch them; then Thomas exclaimed: "My Lord and my God!" (Jn 20:28). So Jesus said: "Have you believed because you have seen me? Blessed are those who have not seen and yet believe" (v. 29); and who were those who believed without seeing? Other disciples, other men and women of Jerusalem, who, on the testimony of the Apostles and the women, believed, even though they had not met the Risen Jesus. This is a very important word about faith, we can call it *the beatitude of faith*.

Pope Francis, *Regina Coeli*
St. Peter's Square, April 7, 2013

Pentecost

Acts 2:1–13

When the time for Pentecost was fulfilled, they were all in one place together. And suddenly there came from the sky a noise like a strong driving wind, and it filled the entire house in which they were. Then there appeared to them tongues as of fire, which parted and came to rest on each one of them. And they were all filled with the holy Spirit and began to speak in different tongues, as the Spirit enabled them to proclaim.

Now there were devout Jews from every nation under heaven staying in Jerusalem. At this sound, they gathered in a large crowd, but they were confused because each one heard them speaking in his own language. They were astounded, and in amazement they asked, "Are not all these people who are speaking Galileans? Then how does each of us hear them in his own native language? We are Parthians, Medes, and Elamites, inhabitants of Mesopotamia, Judea and Cappadocia, Pontus and Asia, Phrygia and Pamphylia, Egypt and the districts of Libya near Cyrene, as well as travelers from Rome, both Jews and converts to Judaism, Cretans and Arabs, yet we hear them speaking in our own tongues of the mighty acts of God." They were all astounded and bewildered, and said to one another, "What does this mean?" But others said, scoffing, "They have had too much new wine."

Since the second century AD, tradition has attributed Acts of the Apostles to Luke, the author of the third Gospel. His works should be read as continuous because, according to some scholars, these two books were originally a single work. The tone of Luke's writing makes it a historical account, but he is also a believer. Every line he writes not only documents details but also presents an invitation to the reader to decide for or against having faith.

The Protagonists

THE HOLY SPIRIT is the main protagonist of Acts, and that is the case in this passage as well. Invisible but always present, he guides, assists, and encourages the disciples and believers in the fulfillment of their respective missions. Every important action by the Church is made in accordance with the will and guidance of the Holy Spirit. He manifests himself to the Apostles and to the community, especially during community gatherings and prayer. In this passage, the Holy Spirit confirms the Apostles in their work; he anoints them and remains with them permanently. His action is the overwhelming impetus that will lead them to preach soon after.

THE APOSTLES at this time are gathered together in the Upper Room. After the coming of the Holy Spirit, their behavior is completely altered. We see a radical change in the Apostles after the descent of the Spirit: they are new prophets.

THE CROWD displays both amazement and derision at the manifestation of the Spirit.

In Genesis 11:1–9, we find the story of the Tower of Babel, through which the sacred writer explains the existence of different languages. The text tells the story about the attempt by a group of people to defy God, to reach the heavens, "and so make a name for ourselves" (v. 4), and about the way God intervenes to disperse them. The sin attributed to the men is pride; in other words, they are behaving no differently than their ancestors.

On the day of Pentecost, the Spirit comes down on the Apostles, who then begin to speak in all the different languages of the world.

The Greek word "Pentecost" means "fifty days," in this case, fifty days after Passover. The feast originally was a celebration of thanksgiving for the harvest, but it was later enriched with the significance of the renewal of the covenant. It is this second significance that interests Luke, and he designs his narrative to connect this event in Acts to the giving of the Law at Sinai.

The coming of the Spirit at Pentecost comprises one of the theophanies in the New Testament. The word "theophany" means a special way that God manifests and reveals himself. It can be accompanied by thunder, lightning, earthquakes, and in this case, with tongues of fire that come down on those present. Verse 2 notes the unexpected noise of a strong wind (a sign of the Holy Spirit) and the presence of fire; thunder and smoke are part of the theophany in Exodus 19:16–19.

The author of Acts seems to be describing this scene by modeling it on that Old Testament event, as though this is a renewal of the covenant. There was a great need for a renewal of that covenant. On this occasion, those who are binding themselves to God are Israelites, who become the people of the Lord through this event. As a consequence, all the other nations on earth are now considered "no people" (1 Pt 2:10). On this occasion, the proclamation is made by the Apostles, who are the heirs of the ancient patriarchs and have become the heads of the tribes of the new people of Israel, which all people can understand and join.

The Apostles are together in the Upper Room when the fire of the Spirit comes down on them. After the Spirit comes, they begin to speak in other tongues.

At the moment of Jesus' Death on the Cross, the veil of the Temple was split in two, and the glory of God left the Temple. The Holy Spirit, in the form of flames, permanently descends on the Apostles. People's hearts become the dwelling place of the Holy Spirit now.

The Apostles experience a clear example of *glossolalia*—in Greek, *glossa* (language) and *lalia* (speech). *Glossolalia*, or speaking in tongues, is a use of language that is possible through the intervention of the Holy Spirit, in this case, to allow the Apostles to speak and be understood by all the bystanders. What happens here is the very opposite of what took place at the Tower of Babel. The text mentions all the known nations at that time starting from east to west and then north to south.

This procedure is how the author chooses to describe *oikoumene*, that is, all the known nations of the day. However, the meaning of the text goes beyond that to point to the reunification of all nations through the preaching of Christian missionaries. This is the reason that the Church will address all human beings by speaking in whatever language is needed to make itself understood. The first community of Christians begins through the gift of the Spirit: The Church, the family of God's children, is born. For all of them, as well as for all believers throughout all ages until now, faith in the risen Jesus is a great gift. The crowd that gathers around the Apostles is formed by Jews of the diaspora, the Jews scattered throughout the world who had come to Jerusalem for the feast. They are astonished at the Apostles' words because they can understand them even though they come from all different parts of the world. They hear about God, but the text does not say they believed. Luke reports the perplexity of some and the derision of others who thought the Apostles were drunk with new wine.

The ancient Prophets of Israel experienced very unusual ecstasies that could lead people to believe they were drunk or were having epileptic seizures.

The people hear talk about God but do not succeed in correctly perceiving what is going on. Peter has not yet given them the right key to interpret what is happening. There always needs to be an interpretation of a prophetic manifestation to explain what is occurring and what God is intending to communicate. It will be Peter himself, who is in charge of the Twelve, who will give the interpretation. (See the text from Acts 2 on pp. 100–101). This situation also demonstrates that the charism of speaking in tongues, a gift of the Holy Spirit, is not enough by itself: The Apostles (and their successors) need to interpret it and oversee it.

Rereading the Text Together

After Jesus' Ascension, the Apostles feel abandoned and are afraid of reactions from the Jewish community and the Romans.

On the day of the Jewish feast of Pentecost, fifty days after Passover, the Apostles are together in the Upper Room to pray and celebrate that feast together.

They sincerely believe Jesus is risen, but it is one thing to know the truth in one's head and another to have the courage to bear witness to it.

While they are praying, small tongues of fire come down on them. This profoundly changes them, infusing in them the power not only to sustain their faith but also to give testimony about the Gospel of the risen Christ.

Through the gift of the Holy Spirit, the Apostles receive the power to be faithful to Jesus and to obey his call: "Go, therefore, and make disciples of all nations, baptizing them in the name of the Father, and of the Son, and of the holy Spirit" (Mt 28:19).

For Reflection Together

- The initial behavior of the Apostles is somewhat perplexing. After having experienced Jesus as risen and alive, after receiving his explanations for things he had said earlier, and after witnessing his Ascension, they do not feel any urgency to do what he had commanded them to do: go, preach, and baptize. They needed the fiery intervention of the Holy Spirit. The first sign of the action of the Holy Spirit is the fact that they cannot hold back their words and begin to preach.
- The phenomenon of *glossolalia* often caused problems in the early Christian communities; the people were sometimes more interested in that strange, miraculous, mysterious fact than they were in the fruit of the Spirit. As the result of the action of the Holy Spirit at Pentecost, we see the bystanders are able to understand what the Apostles are saying. What does this make you think of? What are the ways that could be used today to evangelize people?
- The people who hear the Apostles preach come from all over the known world. However, the real foreigner today is not only the person who lives far away geographically but also the one who is far away mentally and morally. What are the cultural and moral environments that Christians are called to evangelize in today?
- The Holy Spirit's infilling of the Apostles gives them the zeal to preach. The presence of the Holy Spirit is promised to the Church in every age and every place and always leads baptized believers to preach. Would you like to comment on these statements?

For Deeper Reflection

On the day of Pentecost when the seven weeks of Easter had come to an end, Christ's Passover is fulfilled in the outpouring of the Holy Spirit, manifested, given, and communicated as a divine person: of his fullness, Christ, the Lord, pours out the Spirit in abundance.

On that day, the Holy Trinity is fully revealed. Since that day, the Kingdom announced by Christ has been open to those who believe in him: in the humility of the flesh and in faith, they already share in the communion of the Holy Trinity. By his coming, which never ceases, the Holy Spirit causes the world to enter into the "last days," the time of the Church, the Kingdom already inherited though not yet consummated.

Catechism of the Catholic Church, no. 731–732

━ ━ ━ ━ ━ ━ ━ ━ ━ ━ ━ ━ ━ ━ ━ ━

The Holy Spirit is the One who makes us recognize the Lord in Christ and prompts us to speak the profession of the Church's faith: "Jesus is Lord" (cf. 1 Cor 12:3b). "Lord" is the title attributed to God in the Old Testament, a title that in the interpretation of the Bible replaced his unpronounceable name. The *Creed* of the Church is nothing other than the development of what we say with this simple affirmation: "Jesus is Lord." Concerning this profession of faith St. Paul tells us that it is precisely a matter of the word and work of the Spirit. If we want to be in the Spirit, we must adhere to this *Creed*. By making it our own, by accepting it as our word we gain access to the work of the Holy Spirit. The words "Jesus is Lord" can be interpreted in two ways. They mean: Jesus is God, and, at the same time: God is Jesus. The Holy Spirit illuminates this reciprocity: Jesus has divine dignity and God has the human face of Jesus. God shows himself in Jesus and by doing so gives us the truth about ourselves. Letting ourselves be enlightened by this word in the depths of our inmost being is the event of Pentecost. In reciting the *Creed* we enter into the mystery of the first Pentecost: a radical transformation results from the tumult of Babel, from those voices yelling at each other: multiplicity becomes a multifaceted unity, understanding grows from the unifying power of the Truth. In the *Creed*—which unites us from all the corners of the earth and which, through the Holy Spirit, ensures that we understand each other even in the diversity of languages—the new community of God's Church is formed through faith, hope and love.

Pope Benedict XVI, Homily
Vatican Basilica, June 12, 2011

The Calling of Paul

Acts 9:1–12, 15–20, 23–26

Now Saul, still breathing murderous threats against the disciples of the Lord, went to the high priest and asked him for letters to the synagogues in Damascus, that, if he should find any men or women who belonged to the Way, he might bring them back to Jerusalem in chains. On his journey, as he was nearing Damascus, a light from the sky suddenly flashed around him. He fell to the ground and heard a voice saying to him, "Saul, Saul, why are you persecuting me?" He said, "Who are you, sir?" The reply came, "I am Jesus, whom you are persecuting. Now get up and go into the city and you will be told what you must do." The men who were traveling with him stood speechless, for they heard the voice but could see no one. Saul got up from the ground, but when he opened his eyes he could see nothing; so they led him by the hand and brought him to Damascus. For three days he was unable to see, and he neither ate nor drank.

There was a disciple in Damascus named Ananias, and the Lord said to him in a vision, "Ananias." He answered, "Here I am, Lord." The Lord said to him, "Get up and go to the street called Straight and ask at the house of Judas for a man from Tarsus named Saul. He is there praying, and [in a vision] he has seen a man named Ananias. . . . Go, for this man is a chosen instrument of mine to carry my name before Gentiles, kings, and Israelites, and I will show him what he will have to suffer for my name." So Ananias went and entered the house; laying his hands on him, he said, "Saul, my brother, the Lord has sent me, Jesus who appeared to you on the way by which you came, that you may regain your sight and be filled with the holy Spirit." Immediately things like scales fell from his eyes and he regained his sight. He got up and was baptized, and when he had eaten, he recovered his strength.

He stayed some days with the disciples in Damascus, and he began at once to proclaim Jesus in the synagogues, that he is the Son of God. . . .

After a long time had passed, the Jews conspired to kill him, but their plot became known to Saul. Now they were keeping watch on the gates day and night so as to kill him, but his disciples took him one night and let him down through an opening in the wall, lowering him in a basket.

When he arrived in Jerusalem he tried to join the disciples, but they were all afraid of him, not believing that he was a disciple.

The author of Acts recounts the history of the organization and preaching of the first Christian community and of the Apostles, especially Peter and Paul. Paul was born in Tarsus in Cilicia (an area in modern Turkey) of a wealthy Jewish family that traded with the East. He was a Roman citizen by birth, and he had a Hebrew-Greek name, Saul-Paul. He described himself as a Jew with Hebrew ancestors of the tribe of Benjamin and as a Pharisee with regard to the Law. From his youth, Paul was sent to Jerusalem by his father to complete his studies under Gamaliel the Elder. In Jerusalem, he became well respected for his knowledge of the Law. We do not know if he knew Jesus.

The Protagonists

PAUL, whose Roman name means "small," is not physically described in this text. He is quite an unusual person. He is presented by the author as a passionate believer. As an observant Jew, he has done all he could for his faith, even persecuting Christians, but when he is converted, he acts on behalf of Christ with the very same intensity. He is described as an "instrument" in verse 15, someone God can use to act in history. He will consider himself merely a servant because he does only what his Master commands him to do. Once Paul is filled with the Spirit, he can do nothing less than preach and throws himself headlong into that mission.

ANANIAS. We do not know about either his age or appearance. We do know that Jesus told him to help Paul. Ananias wanted nothing to do with Paul because he considered him dangerous. However, Ananias undergoes a change; although he is rather dubious and fearful at first, like a true disciple, he decides to do what he is told.

THE MEN WITH PAUL. We know nothing about them, how many of them there were, what their names were, or what they looked like. Their presence is important because they are witnesses that Paul is not having sunstroke on the road to Damascus but that something is really happening to him. They hear a voice although they do not see anything.

THE JEWS who had found a great supporter and a help in Paul now want to kill him, so he is forced to flee at night and is lowered over the wall in a basket.

THE DISCIPLES AND THE APOSTLES who, in the beginning, fear due to Paul's record. It is only the testimony of Barnabas that ensures that they overcome the fear and accept Paul.

JESUS, HOWEVER, IS THE MAIN PROTAGONIST. He is the one who acts and causes others to act. He is the one who calls Paul and Ananias; he is the one who chooses who his disciples are and who will go preach. It is Jesus' intervention and the descent of the Holy Spirit that make Paul become an ardent preacher of the Gospel.

Luke gives us three accounts of Paul's calling (see Acts 9:3–7, 22:6–11, 26:12–18). Paul also gives us a description of that event in Galatians (1:12–16).

The "Way" Luke talks about in verse 2 of Acts, chapter 9, refers to the path followed by the first Christian community. Christ himself is "the Way" for Christians, so following the Way means following Jesus.

Paul is presented as a terrifying adversary who does not give any respite to Christians and persecutes them wherever he goes. He will later dedicate himself to the proclamation of the Gospel with that very same zeal.

In verse 4, we read that the One who is manifesting himself in the light addresses Paul directly and uses his Hebrew name, "Saul." This is an intensely personal expe-

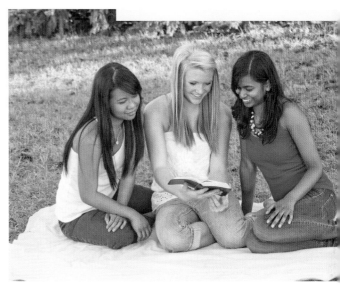

rience. In verse 7, the men with him hear the voice too, which proves that Paul is not imagining things, but they do not see anyone. Something has really happened here, and it concerns Paul in particular. Following the vision, Paul becomes blind, and his condition lasts for three days.

In verse 10, the scene shifts to Damascus to a man there called Ananias. He is told by the Lord about the presence of this man who is highly danger-

ous for Christians, but Jesus wants to use him nonetheless. Paul is referred to as an "instrument" (v. 15). In the Bible, God often intervenes directly in history, but just as frequently, he works through people to get things done.

Ananias is also called by name by the Lord (v. 10) and is entrusted with the mission of welcoming and taking care of Saul-Paul and confirming him in his calling.

Paul is filled with the Holy Spirit (v. 17). His teaching will be as powerful as Peter's because he too has now received the Holy Spirit, the same Spirit who affects people in such a way that they can no longer hold back their words. Paul is baptized (v. 18), and we learn in verse 20 that he immediately begins to preach despite the serious risk to his life.

Fleeing Damascus in a rather inglorious way, Paul goes to the Apostles to tell them what happened, why he has changed, and what he is teaching

Rereading the Text Together

One day, when Paul is going to Damascus to arrest some Christians, Christ appears to him, and as a result Paul becomes blind.

A disciple in Damascus called Ananias visits Paul and baptizes him. It is interesting to note that Ananias was decidedly quite reluctant about the request in his vision to go to Paul. This highlights the terror that the future Apostle to the Gentiles had been causing the Christians.

This text recounts not only Paul's calling but also that of Ananias. Jesus entrusts this disciple with the task of accepting, healing, evangelizing, and baptizing Paul.

Paul—who knew the Scriptures and received a direct calling from Jesus in a vision—still needs to hear the proclamation from a person in the community. He still needs someone to explain to him that his experience is not simply the result of fantasy or a physical condition but is an intervention by the Lord himself.

Anybody in this kind of situation needs an interpretation to understand what he or she is experiencing. In this case, the explanation reaches Paul through the community.

Paul cannot do everything by himself, so he needs to join the community he had persecuted so much. He needs to receive the Spirit, be baptized, and go to the Apostles so as to be able to preach openly.

The same fervor he applied to the persecution of Christians is now used in his dedication to preaching after he is baptized. Because he was such a bitter enemy of the followers of the Gospel before, the early Christians obviously fear his presence in their community.

Paul also wants to go to Jerusalem to present himself to the Apostles and place himself under their authority. He then begins the preaching that will take him around the Roman Empire during his three great missionary journeys.

We know from other documents besides Acts that Paul was arrested and jailed in Jerusalem, but being a Roman citizen, he appealed to the emperor's tribunal. He was then taken to Rome, where he died, probably in AD 67, during the reign of Nero.

For Reflection Together

- Carefully read the long text.
- Try to focus on the various figures involved, their actions, and their words. Reread the text several times so that you remember it well.
- An extraordinary event in Paul's life leads him to faith in Jesus. In every person's life, coming to faith is linked to something particular—an event, a person. Reflect on your own life and try to remember when you decided to become a Christian.
- Perhaps your family always brought you up in the faith. Nevertheless, faith involves a personal commitment and decision, so where are you on this spectrum?

- Paul and Ananias each receive a personal call and are instruments in God's hands. Today people often say that God does not intervene in daily affairs. Believers know, however, that God uses the actions of those who are committed to working in his vineyard. What calling do you think you have received? How do you intend to be an instrument of God's action?

For Deeper Reflection

Such is not the case for Simon Peter when he confesses Jesus as "the Christ, the Son of the living God" (Mt 16:16) for Jesus responds solemnly: "Flesh and blood has not *revealed* this to you, but *my Father* who is in heaven" (Mt 16:17). Similarly Paul will write, regarding his conversion on the road to Damascus, "When he who had set me apart before I was born, and had called me through his grace, was pleased to reveal his Son to me, in order that I might preach him among the Gentiles . . . " (Gal 1:15–16). "And in the synagogues immediately [Paul] proclaimed Jesus, saying, 'He is the Son of God'" (Acts 9:20). From the beginning this acknowledgment of Christ's divine sonship will be the center of the apostolic faith, first professed by Peter as the Church's foundation.

Catechism of the Catholic Church, no. 442

In the ancient Church Baptism was also called "illumination," because this Sacrament gives light; it truly makes one see. In Paul what is pointed out theologically was also brought about physically: healed of his inner blindness, he sees clearly. Thus St. Paul was not transformed by a thought but by an event, by the irresistible presence of the Risen One whom subsequently he would never be able to doubt, so powerful had been the evidence of the event, of this encounter. It radically changed Paul's life in a fundamental way; in this sense one can and must speak of a conversion. This encounter is the center of St. Luke's account for which it is very probable that he used an account that may well have originated in the community of Damascus. This is suggested by the local color, provided by Ananias' presence and by the names, of both the street and the owner of the house in which Paul stayed (Acts 9: 11).

Pope Benedict XVI, General Audience
Paul VI Audience Hall, September 3, 2008

The *Kerygma*

1 Cor 15:1–8, 12–19

Now I am reminding you, brothers, of the gospel I preached to you, which you indeed received and in which you also stand. Through it you are also being saved, if you hold fast to the word I preached to you, unless you believed in vain. For I handed on to you as of first importance what I also received: that Christ died for our sins in accordance with the scriptures; that he was buried; that he was raised on the third day in accordance with the scriptures; that he appeared to Cephas, then to the Twelve. After that, he appeared to more than five hundred brothers at once, most of whom are still living, though some have fallen asleep. After that he appeared to James, then to all the apostles. Last of all, as to one born abnormally, he appeared to me. . . .

But if Christ is preached as raised from the dead, how can some among you say there is no resurrection of the dead? If there is no resurrection of the dead, then neither has Christ been raised. And if Christ has not been raised, then empty [too] is our preaching; empty, too, your faith. Then we are also false witnesses to God, because we testified against God that he raised Christ, whom he did not raise if in fact the dead are not raised. For if the dead are not raised, neither has Christ been raised, and if Christ has not been raised, your faith is vain; you are still in your sins. Then those who have fallen asleep in Christ have perished. If for this life only we have hoped in Christ, we are the most pitiable people of all.

G The *kerygma*, meaning "message," or "proclamation" in Greek, is the initial message of the Resurrection of Jesus.

Paul generally preached in the most important central cities where it was easier to encounter many people. In all the commercial centers of the regions that overlook the Mediterranean, there were Jewish communities of various sizes. Wherever Paul arrived, he would attend the services in the synagogue on the Sabbath. As a visiting guest, he was offered the opportunity to comment on the sacred readings. This was an excellent occasion to proclaim the Gospel of Jesus, but it brought division inside the Jewish community, and he was very often driven out. At this point, Paul began preaching to the pagans. Those who believed the proclamation of the Gospel were baptized, and then a Christian community was formed. Paul would stay for a while with the new believers to deepen their teaching and to organize the life of the community. Paul generally chose responsible members of the group to guide the new group of believers, and then he would move on to another city.

Paul's work was fundamental for the early Christian community. He is correctly called the "Apostle to the Gentiles" (the non-Jews were called *goyim*). He went on three long missionary journeys in Asia Minor and Greece, founding dozens of communities. Paul maintained frequent communication with the different churches, whether through the people he sent or through the letters he wrote to the communities that turned to him for advice and explanations about the faith.

An expert in Jewish culture, Paul was also very knowledgeable about Greco-Roman culture and was able to present the Christian message in an authentic and effective way. Up to that point, the message had been lived out and practiced only in Jewish environments. Paul knew how to talk about the Gospel of Jesus, whether to the people of ancient Israel or to the pagans.

Verses 3b–5 of Paul's First Letter to the Corinthians, chapter 15, contain enormous riches that have been left to us as an inheritance from the early Christians, the very ones who taught it to Paul. We need to be grateful to Paul as well that he transmitted these words and their profound content in a simple way. Paul intends to focus the reader's attention—and that of the hearers too, since his letters were read to the community—on the fundamental elements of Christian faith:

- Christ has died,
- for our sins,
- according to the Scriptures.
- He was buried.
- He was raised on the third day.
- He appeared to Cephas,
- then to the Twelve,
- and then to more than five hundred brothers at once.
- He appeared to James.
- He also appeared to Paul.
- Paul transmitted what he received. "Transmit" and "receive" are verbs that indicate the relationship between a teacher (who transmits) and a student (who receives). Within the Church, the Gospel needs to be both transmitted and received.
- The Gospel is able to bring salvation if it is preached in its entirety and is not modified to suit people's preferences.
- Whoever does not believe in Jesus' Resurrection believes in vain.

Paul's logic is very linear in terms of facts:

- Jesus died and was buried.
- After three days, he was raised up (by God).

At this point, he brings in eyewitnesses:

- He appeared to Cephas, James, the Twelve, five hundred people, and himself. (Paul's implication is that people can talk to these eyewitnesses and ask what happened.)

Paul also refers to the Scriptures to say that this was foreseen and is therefore not something extraneous but central to God's plan of salvation.

Rereading the Text Together

Please read the whole text again so that you can follow the commentary more easily. You could also read all of chapter 15 of the Letter.

▶

Paul writes to people living in Corinth. They do not have a problem determining what the most important part of Christian faith is since they already believe in Jesus' Resurrection. Their major questions do not revolve around Jesus' Resurrection but around their own resurrection. Insofar as Jesus is God, it was reasonable from their point of view that Jesus was resurrected, but they get stuck at the point where they need to believe that the same thing will occur for all human beings. In responding to their query, Paul also helps us understand an important point. If there is no resurrection for human beings, then Christ has not been resurrected, and therefore Christians would believe in him in vain! Resurrection is thus the foundational element of faith.

This document from Paul is very important because verses 3b–5 are very ancient and are part of the ancient formula of faith that Paul himself committed to memory, which we can tell from the rhythm of his words. That wording was probably developed around AD 34, whereas the text of Acts, chapter 2 (in the next section), if it dates back to Peter, could have arisen in AD 32. This means that, from the very first years after Jesus' Death and Resurrection, this is the creed of the early community, and it has remained unchanged until our day. Only the person who believes that Christ is risen can call himself or herself a Christian.

For Deeper Reflection

What does it mean that Jesus is risen? It means that the love of God is stronger than evil and death itself; it means that the love of God can transform our lives and let those desert places in our hearts bloom. The love of God can do this!

This same love for which the Son of God became man and followed the way of humility and self-giving to the very end, down to hell—to the abyss of separation from God—this same merciful love has flooded with light the dead body of Jesus, has transfigured it, has made it pass into eternal life. Jesus did not return to his former life, to earthly life, but entered into the glorious life of God and he entered there with our humanity, opening us to a future of hope.

This is what Easter is: it is the exodus, the passage of human beings from slavery to sin and evil to the freedom of love and goodness. Because God is life, life alone, and we are his glory: the living man (cf. Irenaeus, *Adversus Haereses* [*Against Heresies*], 4, 20, 5–7).

Dear brothers and sisters, Christ died and rose once for all, and for everyone, but the power of the Resurrection, this passover from slavery to evil to the freedom of goodness, must be accomplished in every age, in our concrete existence, in our everyday lives.

Pope Francis, *Urbi et Orbi*
Easter Message, March 31, 2013

THE PROMISE OF THE HOLY SPIRIT

Acts 2:14–16, 22–36

Then Peter stood up with the Eleven, raised his voice, and proclaimed to them, "You who are Jews, indeed all of you staying in Jerusalem. Let this be known to you, and listen to my words. These people are not drunk, as you suppose, for it is only nine o'clock in the morning. No, this is what was spoken through the prophet Joel:

> 'It will come to pass in the last days,' God says,
> > 'that I will pour out a portion of my spirit
> > upon all flesh.
> Your sons and your daughters shall prophesy,
> > your young men shall see visions,
> > your old men shall dream dreams. . . .'

You who are Israelites, hear these words. Jesus the Nazorean was a man commended to you by God with mighty deeds, wonders, and signs, which God worked through him in your midst, as you yourselves know. This man, delivered up by the set plan and foreknowledge of God, you killed, using lawless men to crucify him. But God raised him up, releasing him from the throes of death, because it was impossible for him to be held by it. For David says of him:

> 'I saw the Lord ever before me,
> > with him at my right hand I shall not be disturbed.
> Therefore my heart has been glad and my tongue has exulted;
> > my flesh, too, will dwell in hope,
> because you will not abandon my soul to the netherworld,
> > nor will you suffer your holy one to see corruption.
> You have made known to me the paths of life;
> > you will fill me with joy in your presence.'

My brothers, one can confidently say to you about the patriarch David that he died and was buried, and his tomb is in our midst to this day. But since he was a prophet and knew that God had sworn an oath to him that he would set one of his descendants upon his throne, he foresaw and spoke of the resurrection of the Messiah, that neither was he abandoned to the netherworld nor did his flesh see corruption. God raised this Jesus; of this we are all witnesses. Exalted at the right hand of God, he received the promise of the holy Spirit from the Father and poured it forth, as you [both] see and hear. For David did not go up into heaven, but he himself said:

'The Lord said to my Lord,
"Sit at my right hand
until I make your enemies your footstool."'

Therefore let the whole house of Israel know for certain that God has made him both Lord and Messiah, this Jesus whom you crucified."

The
CONTEXT
of the
Passage

The first *kerygmatic* discourse is the explanation by Peter, as head of the Apostles, of what happened immediately after the coming of the Spirit. In the Bible, when the Spirit of the Lord took hold of the prophets, his power was so irresistible that they could do nothing other than speak in God's name.

For Reflection Together

- The two passages we have just read recount the testimonies of Peter and Paul. We are hearing the words of two champions of the mission as we explore the importance of the mission and of being missionaries these days. However, a missionary needs to know what things to say about the Gospel. The two Apostles have said those things clearly. Do you know what the message is?
- Paul states that those who look to Christ only in terms of their earthly lives are wasting their time. Often throughout history, people have tried to make Jesus into just a revolutionary, a prophet, a wise man, a teacher. According to what we have learned from the two passages we have just read, what does Jesus do that is important for human beings?
- What are the consequences of Jesus' Resurrection for human beings?
- Why does Paul refuse to allow people to think that Jesus' Resurrection is unique to him and cannot happen to them?
- Peter uses Scriptures from the Old Testament as a testimony. In what ways can those Scriptures help people to interpret Jesus' experience?

The Spirit gives the gift of prophecy to the Apostles, and they testify that Jesus has risen. None of this happens by accident or because the Apostles are drunk but because it had already been announced beforehand by the Prophets of Israel. Joel had foretold the descent of the Spirit on every Israelite. The people of Israel were even meant to be a people of prophets. This occurrence would be the signal that the Kingdom of God had come.

Peter uses a rabbinical kind of reasoning, a demonstration that is based on a citation from the LXX, the Greek translation of the Bible known as the Septuagint. He uses it as an explanation to support what is happening. He speaks on behalf of the Apostles, affirming that what has happened is an integral part of Israel's tradition. The Old Testament texts that Peter uses as proof play a similar role to the eyewitness testimony about the risen Christ that Paul describes in the passage from 1 Corinthians 15.

The heart of Peter's discourse is the proclamation of the Death and Resurrection of Jesus, whom God has exalted. Jesus was seen by all the people performing powerful signs, miracles, and wonders that should have testified about him because God himself was manifesting his power through Jesus. Israel thought they would recognize the Messiah by certain signs: the dead would be raised, the blind would regain their sight, the dumb would speak, the lame would walk, and the Kingdom of God would be announced to the poor. Although all of this did take place, Jesus was still not recognized and was even handed over to the pagans (the Romans) to be crucified. Peter sets forth a very clear accusation: You handed him over, you crucified him, you killed him (v. 23).

Interpreting recent facts with the help of the Spirit, Peter points to some Old Testament Scriptures and affirms that the Resurrection of Jesus was already announced by David. These particular Scriptures were very important to the first Christian community and were integrated with the accounts of Jesus' life, actions, and words; they interpenetrated each other and shed light on each other.

David was considered a prophet in Israel. God had promised him the permanent establishment of his throne (see 2 Sm 7:16). Seeming to speak of himself, this king had said that he would never die (see Ps 118:17). Everyone knew David died, and they knew exactly where his grave was. However, David was a prophet and was not referring to himself but to one of his descendants, the Messianic King. Jesus is the awaited Messiah. God raised him from the dead since death had no power to hold him, and all the Apostles are witnesses of that fact. Peter affirms that Jesus was lifted up (which can also mean "was removed") and killed, but his tomb was found empty after three days, thus fulfilling David's prophecy.

Just as the people could examine David's tomb, they could go examine Jesus' tomb. While David's tomb contained the king's remains, Jesus' tomb was completely empty.

Rereading the Text Together

In analyzing the passages from Peter's first *kerygmatic* discourse and Paul's letter, we can establish the following facts:

- Christ is risen.
- His Resurrection was foretold by the Scriptures.
- The Apostles proclaimed it.
- They received the Holy Spirit.
- They are now prophets too.

Peter's fundamental message and that of the other Apostles concerns the proclamation that Jesus is risen. In Acts, there are seven other *kerygmatic* discourses. All of the New Testament is a hymn to the Resurrection of Jesus because that is the authentic Gospel ("Good News") brought by the Apostles and the first Christian community.

For Deeper Reflection

"We bring you the good news that what God promised to the fathers, this day he has fulfilled to us their children by raising Jesus" (Acts 13:32–33). The Resurrection of Jesus is the crowning truth of our faith in Christ, a faith believed and lived as the central truth by the first Christian community; handed on as fundamental by Tradition; established by the documents of the New Testament; and preached as an essential part of the Paschal mystery along with the cross:

Christ is risen from the dead!
Dying, he conquered death;
To the dead, he has given life. (Byzantine Liturgy, Troparion of Easter)

The mystery of Christ's resurrection is a real event, with manifestations that were historically verified, as the New Testament bears witness. In about AD 56 St. Paul could already write to the Corinthians: "I delivered to you as of first importance what I also received, that Christ died for our sins in accordance with the scriptures, and that he was buried, that he was raised on the third day in accordance with the scriptures, and that he appeared to Cephas, then to the Twelve. . ." (1 Cor 15:3–4). The Apostle speaks here of the living tradition of the Resurrection which he had learned after his conversion at the gates of Damascus.

Catechism of the Catholic Church, nos. 638–639

Preaching to All Nations

Then the angel of the Lord spoke to Philip, "Get up and head south on the road that goes down from Jerusalem to Gaza, the desert route." So he got up and set out. Now there was an Ethiopian eunuch, a court official of the Candace, that is, the queen of the Ethiopians, in charge of her entire treasury, who had come to Jerusalem to worship, and was returning home. Seated in his chariot, he was reading the prophet Isaiah. The Spirit said to Philip, "Go and join up with that chariot." Philip ran up and heard him reading Isaiah the prophet and said, "Do you understand what you are reading?" He replied, "How can I, unless someone instructs me?" So he invited Philip to get in and sit with him. This was the scripture passage he was reading:

> "Like a sheep he was led to the slaughter,
>> and as a lamb before its shearer is silent,
>>> so he opened not his mouth.
> In [his] humiliation justice was denied him.
>> Who will tell of his posterity?
>> For his life is taken from the earth."

Then the eunuch said to Philip in reply, "I beg you, about whom is the prophet saying this? About himself, or about someone else?" Then Philip opened his mouth and, beginning with this scripture passage, he proclaimed Jesus to him. As they traveled along the road they came to some water, and the eunuch said, "Look, there is water. What is to prevent my being baptized?" Then he ordered the chariot to stop, and Philip and the eunuch both went down into the water, and he baptized him. When they came out of the water, the Spirit of the Lord snatched Philip away, and the eunuch saw him no more, but continued on his way rejoicing. Philip came to Azotus, and went about proclaiming the good news to all the towns until he reached Caesarea.

The Protagonists

PHILIP. The text does not say much about him except that he is faithful to what the angel tells him to do. Philip resembles Joseph in Matthew's Gospel, to some extent, when he likewise receives an invitation from an angel in a dream and immediately does what the angel asks (see Mt 1:20, 24). Philip becomes aware that the other protagonist is an Ethopian eunuch and that he is trying to understand the text of Isaiah he is reading. That specific point is important to Philip.

THE ANGEL is a figure who shows up very briefly. He gives an order and then disappears.

THE ETHIOPIAN. We know quite a lot about his function and his sociological status, but we do not know anything about his name, age, or appearance. The author prefers to concentrate on those details that could interfere with his acceptance as a person: he is a eunuch and a foreigner. The eunuch, who seems to be alone in this passage, undergoes an evolution. From the beginning, he desires to have deeper knowledge of the Scriptures and takes the next step of accepting the Gospel that is preached to him.

THE HOLY SPIRIT IS ACTUALLY THE TRUE PROTAGONIST. He is the one who makes it possible for the Apostle to meet the Ethiopian and guides Philip's preaching. The Holy Spirit makes Philip understand that this man needs to be baptized.

During the first years of the Christian community, there was no clear demarcation between the Christians and the Jews. The new group could even have been considered as one of the various religious sects within the Jewish community.

Obviously, the Jews had no interest in knowing Christians since they considered them as members of another religion. As for the Christians, they continued to consider themselves part of the Jewish community that observed the Law, even if it was interpreted in the light of Jesus' teaching, and they attended synagogues and went to the Temple.

The understanding of what had really happened with Jesus and of what the community should do dawned only gradually. One of the fundamental points concerned evangelization. They wondered if the message of Jesus' Resurrection was meant for everybody or if it was a privilege afforded only to those who already belonged to the people of Israel.

This issue will be resolved at the Council of Jerusalem.

In the meantime, there are many important episodes recorded in Acts that bring out all the complexity of this issue but also its rich significance. One of these is the episode in which Philip meets the eunuch, and a later episode involves the Apostle Peter, when he is sent by the Holy Spirit to preach the Gospel to Cornelius.

Your
INTERACTION
with the
Text

An angel appears in this episode. The Greek word *angelos*, translated as "angel," means a "messenger," someone who brings a message of greeting or of good news. God often uses angels to bring messages to various people, and in Acts, angels are often seen acting in a variety of ways (see Acts 1:10, 5:19, 10:3, 12:7–10, 12:23, 27:23). In the verses that follow, this angel is not mentioned again, but the text speaks of the Spirit who intervenes to direct Philip's actions.

The person Philip is called to evangelize is a eunuch, someone who all the children of Israel thought was unclean, not only because he was Ethiopian and thus part of the Gentiles (the nations, the non-Jews), but also because of his mutilated condition. The Ethiopia referred to here is not present-day Ethiopia but Nubia, situated between the major cataracts of the Nile and the Sudan. It is often referred to as the Kingdom of Kush.

The Holy Spirit, however, prompts Philip to reach out to this man. Philip finds the eunuch reading a section of Isaiah (Is 53:7–8), and he uses this as the starting point to evangelize a man who would not have been welcome in a Jewish community. The Scripture quoted from Isaiah comes from the Greek translation of the Old Testament, the LXX or Septuagint. This was the version generally used by the

Christian community that spoke Greek. The method Philip chooses, a proclamation that begins with a reading from the Old Testament, will be widely followed by the first Christian community.

Accepting Philip's message, the eunuch becomes a believer and gets baptized immediately, since there is water for this sacrament in the area.

Rereading the Text Together

Who has the privilege of entering into the Church? Who can become a Christian? To whom should the Gospel be proclaimed? These questions may seem superfluous, given that we are used to living in a somewhat Christianized environment, although that environment runs the risk of losing its origins. The answer that comes from this passage is clear: no one, not even a foreigner or someone who is bodily maimed, is to be deprived of the right to hear the Gospel. The Spirit who prompts Philip to evangelize and baptize a man who was considered unclean is the same Spirit with us today.

For Reflection Together

- What situation does this passage involve?
- Does the story have any relevance for us today?
- If you were to tell this story with modern characters, what details would change? Who would the people in this episode be?
- What does Philip decide to do?
- What would you have done if you had been in Philip's shoes?
- Who could the Ethiopian be today?
- What prejudices today keep us away from strangers or people we consider different from ourselves?

Cornelius

Acts 10:9–16, 19–48

Peter went up to the roof terrace to pray at about noontime. He was hungry and wished to eat, and while they were making preparations he fell into a trance. He saw heaven opened and something resembling a large sheet coming down, lowered to the ground by its four corners. In it were all the earth's four-legged animals and reptiles and the birds of the sky. A voice said to him, "Get up, Peter. Slaughter and eat." But Peter said, "Certainly not, sir. For never have I eaten anything profane and unclean." The voice spoke to him again, a second time, "What God has made clean, you are not to call profane." This happened three times, and then the object was taken up into the sky. . . .

As Peter was pondering the vision, the Spirit said [to him], "There are three men here looking for you. So get up, go downstairs, and accompany them without hesitation, because I have sent them." Then Peter went down to the men and said, "I am the one you are looking for. What is the reason for your being here?" They answered, "Cornelius, a centurion, an upright and God-fearing man, respected by the whole Jewish nation, was directed by a holy angel to summon you to his house and to hear what you have to say." So he invited them in and showed them hospitality.

The next day he got up and went with them, and some of the brothers from Joppa went with him. On the following day he entered Caesarea. Cornelius was expecting them and had called together his relatives and close friends. When Peter entered, Cornelius met him and, falling at his feet, paid him homage. Peter, however, raised him up, saying, "Get up. I myself am also a human being." While he conversed with him, he went in and found many people gathered together and said to them, "You know that it is unlawful for a Jewish man to associate with, or visit, a Gentile, but God has shown me that I should not call any person profane or unclean. And that is why I came without objection when sent for. May I ask, then, why you summoned me?" Cornelius replied, "Four days ago at this hour, three o'clock in the afternoon, I was at prayer in my house when suddenly a man in dazzling robes stood before me and said, 'Cornelius, your prayer has been heard and your almsgiving remembered before God. Send therefore to Joppa and summon Simon, who is called Peter. He is a guest in the house of Simon, a tanner, by the sea.' So I sent for you immediately, and you were kind enough to come. Now therefore we are all here in the presence of God to listen to all that you have been commanded by the Lord."

Then Peter proceeded to speak and said, "In truth, I see that God shows no partiality. Rather, in every nation whoever fears him and acts uprightly is acceptable to him. You know the word [that] he sent to the Israelites as he proclaimed peace through Jesus Christ, who is Lord of all, what has happened all over Judea, beginning in Galilee after the Baptism that John preached, how God anointed Jesus of Nazareth with the holy Spirit and power. He went about doing good and healing all those oppressed by the devil, for God was with him. We are witnesses of all that he did both in the country of the Jews and [in] Jerusalem. They put him to death by hanging him on a tree. This man God raised [on] the third day and granted that he be visible, not to all the people, but to us, the witnesses chosen by God in advance, who ate and drank with him after he rose from the dead. He commissioned us to preach to the people and testify that he is the one appointed by God as judge of the living and the dead. To him all the prophets bear witness, that everyone who believes in him will receive forgiveness of sins through his name."

While Peter was still speaking these things, the holy Spirit fell upon all who were listening to the word. The circumcised believers who had accompanied Peter were astounded that the gift of the holy Spirit should have been poured out on the Gentiles also, for they could hear them speaking in tongues and glorifying God. Then Peter responded, "Can anyone withhold the water for baptizing these people, who have received the holy Spirit even as we have?" He ordered them to be baptized in the name of Jesus Christ.

Reconstructing exactly how the first Christian communities were formed is rather difficult because of the lack of data. We know that the Hellenistic culture had heavily penetrated the whole region, and in the diaspora, many pagans had come to believe in the faith of the patriarchs and became proselytes who were referred to as "God-fearing." Among these pagan sympathizers who renounced polytheism, there were some who sought to be completely assimilated into Judaism and became "proselytes of righteousness," a status attained through circumcision and a purification rite. With circumcision, the proselyte was incorporated into the Jewish people with full rights and responsibilities. However, this practice was not widely followed or accepted for two reasons. The ritual operation of circumcision itself was unappealing; there was a certain repugnance and derision of adult male nudity for any reason (including nude males competing in sports). Secondly, acceptance of all the statutes for cleanliness would automatically lead to cutting ties to someone's social environment. In addition, the observance of the commandments that guided the religious life of the patriarch Noah, especially the prohibition of consuming blood (see Gn 9:4), assured salvation for those who were not circumcised. The group of the God-fearing was large and had a good understanding of the Septuagint.

To understand this passage, it is helpful to remember that not all animals were appropriate for the diet of Jews, who could eat the flesh only of animals with a cloven hoof that chew the cud (sheep, goats, and cows). Pigs were prohibited because, although they have a cloven hoof, they do not chew the cud. In addition, the animals had to be slaughtered according to very precise rules by an expert butcher and completely drained of blood. In the past, the *goyim* (non-Jews) would kill the animal through strangulation, and a Jew would not have been able to eat that meat.

The Protagonists

PETER. We know from the New Testament that Peter has a volatile personality and often speaks without thinking, so what he says can range from the sublime to the highly inappropriate. However, the author of Acts shows him unusually cautious here. We know from historical reconstructions that Peter would not have favored Baptism for pagans unless they accepted circumcision as well. Peter is a traditionalist who needs a direct vision before he can consent to enlarging the boundaries of the Church, of which he is the custodian and guarantor. (It is Paul who first understands that knowledge of the Gospel is meant for everyone and that circumcision should not be imposed on non-Jews.) Three times Peter is told to eat of the animals in the sheet. In the end he yields, but he understands what the vision means only when he sees that the Holy Spirit has come upon Cornelius.

CORNELIUS is presented in this text as someone who is faithful to God's will. He does whatever he is told to do. The evident sign that Cornelius' actions are approved by God is the presence of the Spirit resting upon him.

THE HOLY SPIRIT, HOWEVER, IS THE MAIN PROTAGONIST. He sends the vision to Peter, he communicates with Cornelius, and he is the one who provides Peter with an understanding of what is transpiring and what he is being asked to do.

This passage recounts the episode in which an angel appeared to Cornelius, a Roman centurion who feared God and whose family followed his religious sentiments and convictions. The angel prompted him to send for Peter, who was staying with Simon, a tanner in Jaffa. Cornelius followed the angel's bidding and sent two servants to Peter, but as they were approaching, Peter had a vision too.

A sheet was lowered before his eyes that contained every kind of animal. A voice invited Peter to kill and eat these animals, but Peter did not obey because those animals were unclean. Three separate times, Peter refused the invitation because he was a good Jew and would never for any reason have transgressed a law that was so deep-rooted among his people. Three times, he heard the voice that said, "What God has made clean, you are not to call profane."

Rereading the Text Together

Peter's experience is even more significant than Philip's. While he was having the vision, Peter did not know its intended meaning, but while he was reflecting on its significance, Cornelius' two servants arrived. Without the vision, Peter would most probably not have agreed to go to Cornelius' house. Instead, he went to preach to him and his family, and while he was preaching, the Holy Spirit came down on all those who were present. This event was decisive for Peter to discern the right path forward. He could not deny Baptism to people who had already received the same Holy Spirit that the Apostles had received.

For Deeper Reflection

From the very day of Pentecost the Church has celebrated and administered holy Baptism. Indeed St. Peter declares to the crowd astounded by his preaching: "Repent, and be baptized every one of you in the name of Jesus Christ for the forgiveness of your sins; and you shall receive the gift of the Holy Spirit" (Acts 2:38). The apostles and their collaborators offer Baptism to anyone who believed in Jesus: Jews, the God-fearing, pagans. Always, Baptism is seen as connected with faith: "Believe in the Lord Jesus, and you will be saved, you and your household," St. Paul declared to his jailer in Philippi. And the narrative continues, the jailer "was baptized at once, with all his family" (Acts 16:31, 33).

Catechism of the Catholic Church, no. 1226

The Acts of the Apostles describe the episode of Cornelius, a centurion of the Italic cohort, as a crucial stage for the entry of the Gospel into the Gentile world. On a command from God, Cornelius sent someone to fetch Peter and Peter, also following a divine command, went to the centurion's house and preached there. While he was speaking the Holy Spirit descended on the domestic community that had gathered and Peter said: "Can anyone forbid water for baptizing these people who have received the Holy Spirit just as we have?" (Acts 10:47). Thus at the Council of Jerusalem, Peter became the intercessor for the Church of the Gentiles who had no need of the Law because God had "cleansed their hearts by faith" (Acts 15:9). Of course, in the Letter to the Galatians Paul says God empowered Peter for the apostolic ministry among the circumcised, and instead empowered him, Paul, for the ministry to the Gentiles (2:8). This assignment however could only be in force while Peter remained with the Twelve in Jerusalem in the hope that all Israel would adhere to Christ. As they faced the further development, the Twelve recognized when it was time for them too to set out for the whole world to proclaim the Gospel. Peter who, complying with God's order, had been the first to open the door to pagans, now left the leadership of the Christian-Jewish Church to James the Lesser in order to dedicate himself to his true mission: the ministry for the unity of the one Church of God formed by Jews and pagans. Among the Church's characteristics, St. Paul's desire to go to Rome places emphasis—as we have seen—on the word "*catholic*." St. Peter's journey to Rome, as representative of the world's peoples, comes especially under the word "*one*": his task was to create the *unity* of the *catholica*, the Church formed by Jews and pagans, the Church of all the peoples. And this is Peter's ongoing mission: to ensure that the Church is never identified with a single nation, with a single culture or with a single State but is always the Church of all; to ensure that she reunites humanity over and above every boundary and, in the midst of the divisions of this world, makes God's peace present, the reconciling power of his love.

Pope Benedict XVI, Homily
Vatican Basilica, June 29, 2008

The Life of the Community

Acts 2:37–47

Now when they heard this, they were cut to the heart, and they asked Peter and the other apostles, "What are we to do, my brothers?" Peter [said] to them, "Repent and be baptized, every one of you, in the name of Jesus Christ for the forgiveness of your sins; and you will receive the gift of the holy Spirit. For the promise is made to you and to your children and to all those far off, whomever the Lord our God will call." He testified with many other arguments, and was exhorting them, "Save yourselves from this corrupt generation." Those who accepted his message were baptized, and about three thousand persons were added that day.

They devoted themselves to the teaching of the apostles and to the communal life, to the breaking of the bread and to the prayers. Awe came upon everyone, and many wonders and signs were done through the apostles. All who believed were together and had all things in common; they would sell their property and possessions and divide them among all according to each one's need. Every day they devoted themselves to meeting together in the temple area and to breaking bread in their homes. They ate their meals with exultation and sincerity of heart, praising God and enjoying favor with all the people. And every day the Lord added to their number those who were being saved.

For Reflection Together

- As you can see from this passage, the community in Jerusalem had a particular lifestyle. In thinking about the life you are living in the Church, does it seem similar to the one described by the author of Acts? What could be done to make our communities more like the ideal model of the Church that is presented to us there?
- Rereading the text, try to distinguish the major points about the life of this community. Now compare this intense Christian life with yours. What common features do you find? What things would you need to change?
- The passage affirms that the Christians devoted themselves to listening to the teaching of the Apostles. Does it seem to you that this is happening today? What should Christians do today to have that same kind of persistent devotion?

Jesus was born in Bethlehem, and for much of his life he lived in a small village in Galilee, Capernaum. At that time, this region was on the margins of the Roman Empire. During his life, Jesus made only occasional visits outside his home area and did not travel much, usually going only as far as Jerusalem. The Apostles, disciples, and those who accepted his teaching were generally not the elite but common people. At Jesus' Death, his followers were few, and almost all of them lived in Galilee. Little by little, the Gospel of Jesus spread around Jerusalem in Judea. It was then taken north to Samaria and past Galilee. In the end, it left the historical borders of the Jewish nation and spread to the pagan world. The first great pagan city in which a Christian community was formed was Antioch in Syria. From there, through Paul's work, it spread throughout Syria, Asia Minor, and Greece and reached as far as Rome, the capital of the empire and the center of the known world. The way in which the Church spread is one of the most fascinating topics to study.

The language most used in the Roman Empire was *koiné* Greek, a language known to all the peoples of the empire. This is the language in which the Gospel was preached and the writings of the New Testament were transmitted.

The first community consisted of people belonging to very different social classes: poor and rich could equally enter the Church. Young people, adults, old people, and women had an equal right to enter the community. It often happened that someone who was not yet a Christian would participate in these meetings. As for the Jewish Christians, they attended synagogue services on the Sabbath, where they followed the liturgy (what the Church calls the Liturgy of the Word today). Then, on Sunday, they would spend the Lord's Day together, celebrating what Jesus did at the Last Supper. This is an overview of the life of the very first community in Jerusalem.

The early Christians would meet in their homes for prayer. They would gather after work to hear about Jesus, his works, and his signs. The Scriptures that the converts from Judaism already knew were reread in the light of Jesus' life and teachings.

Verses 42 to 45 describe the communal life of the early Christians. Perhaps Luke is setting forth an ideal vision of community, but when he refers to the sharing of goods, he does not mean just the distribution of material goods but the sharing of what they had received from God, that is, their skills and, above all, their spiritual goods. Communal life also included gathering together around the Apostles and meeting for the breaking of bread, a gesture that recalls the Eucharist and not just a sharing of food. Luke is not aiming at a sociological analysis. What interests him is not the description of an egalitarian society but a description of the Spirit that should rule within the Church.

When the text refers to the breaking of the bread, it recalls the Jewish custom of having the person who presides bless the bread before breaking it and dividing it among those at the table. However, for the early Christians, this also meant the assembling of the community for the Eucharist. Before celebrating the Eucharist, they were most probably used to eating a meal together and praying (see 1 Cor 11:20–34).

Verse 46 tells us that these Christians still went to the Temple in Jerusalem and probably to the synagogue as well. At this point in Church history, the difference between the Jewish and Christian communities was still not clear-cut. However, even though Christians attended Jewish religious services, they still met together at specific times to hear preaching and to break bread. Their affirmation that salvation was assured for those who followed the Gospel was clear. Verse 47 speaks of God's action in raising up new believers to enter the community as part of "those who were being saved." Given this context, the early Church identified itself with the rest of Israel, meaning, with the best part of the populace, the people who had remained firm in their faith in God and, for that reason, had continued to be preserved by God throughout every trial.

Rereading the Text Together

The duties of the Christian community were as follows:

- A commitment to evangelize. There is no greater gift that a Christian can give someone than the proclamation that Christ is risen. It is primarily the Apostles who preach in this case, but they function as the representatives of the whole Church. All those who accepted the Gospel took on the responsibility of proclaiming it. ▶

- A commitment to hear the Word of God. Many people today call themselves Christians, but they never gather around the leaders of communities to hear the Word of God and to learn the basics of their faith. By contrast, the early Christians often met together with the Apostles to listen to them preach the Gospel and then try to put it into practice in their daily lives.
- Frequent Communion and attendance at prayer. The central moment in the life of the first community (as it is for us as well) is the encounter with God in the Eucharist and prayer. During the Eucharist, the community gathered around the Apostles to celebrate the memorial of the Lord's Supper.
- The sharing of material and spiritual goods.

For Deeper Reflection

The word "catholic" means "universal," in the sense of "according to the totality" or "in keeping with the whole." The Church is catholic in a double sense:

First, the Church is catholic because Christ is present in her. "Where there is Christ Jesus, there is the Catholic Church" (St. Ignatius of Antioch, *Ad Smyrn.* 8, 2). In her subsists the fullness of Christ's body united with its head; this implies that she receives from him "the fullness of the means of salvation" (*Unitatis Redintegratio*, no. 3; *Ad Gentes*, no. 6) which he has willed: correct and complete confession of faith, full sacramental life, and ordained ministry in apostolic succession. The Church was, in this fundamental sense, catholic on the day of Pentecost and will always be so until the day of the Parousia.

Secondly, the Church is catholic because she has been sent out by Christ on a mission to the whole of the human race:

> All men are called to belong to the new People of God. This People, therefore, while remaining one and only one, is to be spread throughout the whole world and to all ages in order that the design of God's will may be fulfilled: he made human nature one in the beginning and has decreed that all his children who were scattered should be finally gathered together as one. . . . The character of universality which adorns the People of God is a gift from the Lord himself whereby the Catholic Church ceaselessly and efficaciously seeks for the return of all humanity and all its goods, under Christ the Head in the unity of his Spirit. (*Lumen Gentium*, no. 13)

Catechism of the Catholic Church, nos. 830–831

Awaiting the *Parousia*

Lk 12:35–48

"Gird your loins and light your lamps and be like servants who await their master's return from a wedding, ready to open immediately when he comes and knocks. Blessed are those servants whom the master finds vigilant on his arrival. Amen, I say to you, he will gird himself, have them recline at table, and proceed to wait on them. And should he come in the second or third watch and find them prepared in this way, blessed are those servants. Be sure of this: if the master of the house had known the hour when the thief was coming, he would not have let his house be broken into. You also must be prepared, for at an hour you do not expect, the Son of Man will come."

Then Peter said, "Lord, is this parable meant for us or for everyone?" And the Lord replied, "Who, then, is the faithful and prudent steward whom the master will put in charge of his servants to distribute [the] food allowance at the proper time? Blessed is that servant whom his master on arrival finds doing so. Truly, I say to you, he will put him in charge of all his property. But if that servant says to himself, 'My master is delayed in coming, and begins to beat the menservants and the maidservants, to eat and drink and get drunk, then that servant's master will come on an unexpected day and at an unknown hour and will punish him severely and assign him a place with the unfaithful. That servant who knew his master's will but did not make preparations nor act in accord with his will shall be beaten severely; and the servant who was ignorant of his master's will but acted in a way deserving of a severe beating shall be beaten only lightly. Much will be required of the person entrusted with much, and still more will be demanded of the person entrusted with more."

Ⓖ *Parousia* is a Greek term that refers to the second coming of our Lord and Savior Jesus Christ at the end of time, "when history and creation will achieve their fulfillment" (*Catechism of the Catholic Church*, Glossary, "Parousia").

For Reflection Together

- Today, as in the past, people sometimes frantically try in bungling ways to know the exact day the world will come to an end. Many resort to fortune-tellers and other such people to find out when they will die in order to try to delay that day. The passage we read states that it is not possible to know when all these things will happen. However, people need to be clear that they will indeed happen. What implications do you see in all this?
- This text calls us to be vigilant. What are the ways in which today's society numbs believers and makes them grow lax in their vigilant expectation of the coming of Jesus?
- Believers need to be found in an attitude of service with their lamps lit. The mention of loins being girded is a detail that is no longer relevant today because clothing has changed, but it means being prepared to move quickly. Try to describe what the attitude of the believers who serve God and their brothers and sisters should be today.
- Believers should not give themselves over to a partying lifestyle. What are today's temptations that go contrary to the discipline that should characterize Christians' lives?
- The master's approval is mentioned in this passage. Are you aware that God will evaluate your actions?

The Jews thought that one day, at the end of time, the "Son of Man" would come to free Israel from oppression and establish the definitive Kingdom of God. This superhuman person of quasi-divine origin would come down to earth in a cloud from heaven and would receive a special assignment concerning salvation directly from God. The people would not know where he came from or who his parents were, but his coming would be announced by spectacular signs.

Your
INTERACTION
with the
Text

The New Testament presents the concept of "*parousia*," meaning, the second coming of Christ before the Last Judgment. The early Christians were expecting this *parousia* to come very shortly. For that reason, many people stopped working and taking care of the most basic affairs because they believed that since the end of the world was approaching, there was no longer any reason to do normal things like working and earning a living. Paul himself often had to intervene to get the community back to work. As time went on, Christians came to understand that this second coming of Christ would certainly happen, but it coincided with the death of each person as well as with the end of the world, and no one could know the precise time of either event.

The whole passage calls us to the need for vigilance, and in verse 35, we are again told that Christ needs to find us with our "loins girded" in an attitude of service with our lamps lit, like the servant who waits for the master at night until he comes and is immediately ready to serve him.

In verse 37, we are told that the servant should not be found unprepared, and we are presented with a master who, surprisingly, will be the one to serve at table those whom he finds ready. Jesus is actually presented as the one who serves first.

The hour the Master returns will be at an unforeseen and unexpected time that no one can predict. His coming can happen in the middle of the night but also in that indefinite time between night and day, the very time in which those who have kept watch are tempted to sleep. This visitation, which should be expected, assured, and desired, runs the risk of being like the arrival of the thief who comes when the house is unguarded and enters by force to rob it. Just as the master would be on guard if he expected thieves, so too the wise servant should remain expectant and vigilant because, even though the exact time is not known, he or she knows with certainty that the time will come.

Verse 42 speaks about a trusted steward. This is a person who has been given authority over all the other servants in the house. He needs to continue to serve his master faithfully and honestly, without yielding to a desire to become relaxed or yielding to carousing, taking advantage of the master's goods, getting drunk, or overeating. It is therefore a major obligation for the Apostles, for those who directly work to administrate the Church, and for those who evangelize to remain faithful and righteous. The punishment will be different at the end for those who knew the Master's will and those who did not know. In fact, those who learned from the outset will bear more responsibility than others.

Rereading the Text Together

When Jesus affirmed he was the Son of Man, many Jews did not believe him because they thought they knew where Jesus came from and who his parents were. Nevertheless, Jesus is the Son of Man that the prophet Daniel had spoken about (see Dn 7:13–14). For Christians, Jesus is precisely that mysterious figure, a man, but much more than a man; he is God, the Lord of the universe and the Savior of the human race. In this passage, the expectation of the second coming of the Lord is very powerful. At a time like today, people seek to know when the Son of Man will come, but Jesus is not subject to people's predictions. The Master will certainly come, but we cannot know when. He will come unexpectedly, at a moment in which he is not awaited, so we need to be more vigilant, especially when fatigue plays nasty tricks on us and our vigilance is overcome by sleep.

The servant must be ready to serve. However, the master in this parable is unusual because, instead of being served, he is the one who gives the good example of being the first to serve the people at table, and so it is with all who are ready for his arrival. The servants need to keep doing their work honestly, remembering that the responsibilities entrusted to the Church are major ones, and the duties that go with those responsibilities are also great. The Master will evaluate those who knew his will and those who did not know it in different ways.

The major points of this passage are vigilance and service. This means that as believers await the second coming of Christ, they should not be inactive but should remain vigilant in doing the work entrusted to them. Christ will surely come in glory, but he comes to believers many times during their lives, and the Christian should always be found in an attitude of service, ready to do the Father's will.

And now, after examining the various aspects of the expectation of Christ's *parousia*, let us ask ourselves: what are the basic convictions of Christians as regards the last things: death, the end of the world? Their first conviction is the certainty that Jesus is Risen and is with the Father and thus is with us forever. And no one is stronger than Christ, for he is with the Father, he is with us. We are consequently safe, free of fear. This was an essential effect of Christian preaching. Fear of spirits and divinities was widespread in the ancient world. Today too, missionaries alongside many good elements in natural religions encounter fear of the spirits, of evil powers that threaten us. Christ lives, he has overcome death, he has overcome all these powers. We live in this certainty, in this freedom, and in this joy. This is the first aspect of our living with regard to the future.

The second is the certainty that Christ is with me. And just as the future world in Christ has already begun, this also provides the certainty of hope. The future is not darkness in which no one can find his way. It is not like this. Without Christ, even today the world's future is dark, and fear of the future is so common. Christians know that Christ's light is stronger and therefore they live with a hope that is not vague, with a hope that gives them certainty and courage to face the future. . . .

Another element in the Pauline teaching on eschatology is the universality of the call to faith which unites Jews and Gentiles, that is, non-Christians, as a sign and an anticipation of the future reality. For this reason we can say that we are already seated in Heaven with Jesus Christ, but to reveal the riches of grace in the centuries to come (Eph 2:6 f.), the *after* becomes a *before*, in order to show the state of incipient fulfillment in which we live. This makes bearable the sufferings of the present time which, in any case, cannot be compared to the future glory (cf. Rom 8:18). We walk by faith, not by sight, and even if we might rather leave the body to live with the Lord, what definitively matters, whether we are dwelling in the body or are far from it, is that we be pleasing to him (cf. 2 Cor 5:7–9).

Pope Benedict XVI, General Audience
St. Peter's Square, November 12, 2008

In the New Testament, the word *basileia* can be translated by "kingship" (abstract noun), "kingdom" (concrete noun) or "reign" (action noun). The Kingdom of God lies ahead of us. It is brought near in the Word incarnate, it is proclaimed throughout the whole Gospel, and it has come in Christ's death and Resurrection. The Kingdom of God has been coming since the Last Supper and, in the Eucharist, it is in our midst. The kingdom will come in glory when Christ hands it over to his Father:

> It may even be . . . that the Kingdom of God means Christ himself, whom we daily desire to come, and whose coming we wish to be manifested quickly to us. For as he is our resurrection, since in him we rise, so he can also be understood as the Kingdom of God, for in him we shall reign. (St. Cyprian, On the Lord's Prayer [*De Dominica oratione*], no. 8)

This petition is "*Marana tha*," the cry of the Spirit and the Bride: "Come, Lord Jesus."

> Even if it had not been prescribed to pray for the coming of the kingdom, we would willingly have brought forth this speech, eager to embrace our hope. In indignation the souls of the martyrs under the altar cry out to the Lord: "O Sovereign Lord, holy and true, how long before you judge and avenge our blood on those who dwell upon the earth?" (Rev 6:10). For their retribution is ordained for the end of the world. Indeed as soon as possible, Lord, may your kingdom come! (Tertullian, On Prayer [*De oratione*], no. 5)

In the Lord's Prayer, "thy kingdom come" refers primarily to the final coming of the reign of God through Christ's return. But, far from distracting the Church from her mission in this present world, this desire commits her to it all the more strongly. Since Pentecost, the coming of that Reign is the work of the Spirit of the Lord who "complete[s] his work on earth and brings us the fullness of grace" (*Roman Missal*, Eucharistic Prayer IV).

Catechism of the Catholic Church, nos. 2816–2818

Loving God and One's Neighbor

1 Jn 4:7–21

Beloved, let us love one another, because love is of God; everyone who loves is begotten by God and knows God. Whoever is without love does not know God, for God is love. In this way the love of God was revealed to us: God sent his only Son into the world so that we might have life through him. In this is love: not that we have loved God, but that he loved us and sent his Son as expiation for our sins. Beloved, if God so loved us, we also must love one another. No one has ever seen God. Yet, if we love one another, God remains in us, and his love is brought to perfection in us.

This is how we know that we remain in him and he in us, that he has given us of his Spirit. Moreover, we have seen and testify that the Father sent his Son as savior of the world. Whoever acknowledges that Jesus is the Son of God, God remains in him and he in God. We have come to know and to believe in the love God has for us.

God is love, and whoever remains in love remains in God and God in him. In this is love brought to perfection among us, that we have confidence on the day of judgment because as he is, so are we in this world. There is no fear in love, but perfect love drives out fear because fear has to do with punishment, and so one who fears is not yet perfect in love. We love because he first loved us. If anyone says, "I love God," but hates his brother, he is a liar; for whoever does not love a brother whom he has seen cannot love God whom he has not seen. This is the commandment we have from him: whoever loves God must also love his brother.

FAITH AND WORKS

Jas 2:14–26

What good is it, my brothers, if someone says he has faith but does not have works? Can that faith save him? If a brother or sister has nothing to wear and has no food for the day, and one of you says to them, "Go in peace, keep warm, and eat well," but you do not give them the necessities of the body, what good is it? So also faith of itself, if it does not have works, is dead.

Indeed someone might say, "You have faith and I have works." Demonstrate your faith to me without works, and I will demonstrate my faith to you from my works. You believe that God is one. You do well. Even the demons believe that and tremble. Do you want proof, you ignoramus, that faith without works is useless? Was not Abraham our father justified by works when he offered his son Isaac upon the altar? You see that faith was active along with his works, and faith was completed by the works. Thus the scripture was fulfilled that says, "Abraham believed God, and it was credited to him as righteousness," and he was called "the friend of God." See how a person is justified by works and not by faith alone. And in the same way, was not Rahab the harlot also justified by works when she welcomed the messengers and sent them out by a different route? For just as a body without a spirit is dead, so also faith without works is dead.

For Deeper Reflection

True, no one has ever seen God as he is. And yet God is not totally invisible to us; he does not remain completely inaccessible. God loved us first . . . and this love of God has appeared in our midst. He has become visible in as much as he "has sent his only Son into the world, so that we might live through him" (1 Jn 4:9). God has made himself visible: in Jesus we are able to see the Father (cf. Jn 14:9). Indeed, God is visible in a number of ways. In the love-story recounted by the Bible, he comes toward us, he seeks to win our hearts, all the way to the Last Supper, to the piercing of his heart on the Cross, to his appearances after the Resurrection and to the great deeds by which, through the activity of the Apostles, he guided the nascent Church along its path. Nor has the Lord been absent from subsequent Church history: he encounters us ever anew, in the men and women who reflect his presence, in his word, in the sacraments, and especially in the Eucharist. In the Church's Liturgy, in her prayer, in the living community of believers, we experience the love of God, we perceive his presence and we thus learn to recognize that presence in our daily lives. He has loved us first and he continues to do so; we too, then, can respond with love. God does not demand of us a feeling which we ourselves are incapable of producing. He loves us, he makes us see and experience his love, and since he has "loved us first," love can also blossom as a response within us.

In the gradual unfolding of this encounter, it is clearly revealed that love is not merely a sentiment. Sentiments come and go. A sentiment can be a marvelous first spark, but it is not the fullness of love. . . . Contact with the visible manifestations of God's love can awaken within us a feeling of joy born of the experience of being loved. But this encounter also engages our will and our intellect. Acknowledgment of the living God is one path toward love, and the "yes" of our will to his will unites our intellect, will and sentiments in the all-embracing act of love. But this process is always open-ended; love is never "finished" and complete; throughout life, it changes and matures, and thus remains faithful to itself. . . .

Love of neighbor is thus shown to be possible in the way proclaimed by the Bible, by Jesus. It consists in the very fact that, in God and with God, I love even the person whom I do not like or even know. This can only take place on the basis of an intimate encounter with God, an encounter which has become a communion of will, even affecting my feelings. Then I learn to look on this other person not simply with my eyes and my feelings, but from the perspective of Jesus Christ. His friend is my friend. . . . Seeing with the eyes of Christ, I can give to others much more than their outward necessities; I can give them the look of love which they crave. Here we see the necessary interplay between love of God and love of neighbor which the *First Letter of John* speaks of with such insistence. If I have no contact whatsoever with God in my life, then I cannot see in the other anything more than the other, and I am incapable of seeing in him the image of God. But if in my life I fail completely to heed others, solely out of a desire to be "devout" and to perform my "religious duties," then my relationship with God will also grow arid. It becomes merely "proper," but loveless. Only my readiness to encounter my neighbor and to show him love makes me sensitive to God as well. Only if I serve my neighbor can my eyes be opened to what God does for me and how much he loves me.

Pope Benedict XVI, *God Is Love*
(*Deus Caritas Est*), nos. 17–18, 2005

Charity in truth, to which Jesus Christ bore witness by his earthly life and especially by his death and resurrection, is the principal driving force behind the authentic development of every person and of all humanity. Love—*caritas*—is an extraordinary force which leads people to opt for courageous and generous engagement in the field of justice and peace. It is a force that has its origin in God, Eternal Love and Absolute Truth. Each person finds his good by adherence to God's plan for him, in order to realize it fully: in this plan, he finds his truth, and through adherence to this truth he becomes free (cf. Jn 8:32). To defend the truth, to articulate it with humility and conviction, and to bear witness to it in life are therefore exacting and indispensable forms of charity. Charity, in fact, "rejoices in the truth" (1 Cor 13:6). All people feel the interior impulse to love authentically: love and truth never abandon them completely, because these are the vocation planted by God in the heart and mind of every human person. The search for love and truth is purified and liberated by Jesus Christ from the impoverishment that our humanity brings to it, and he reveals to us in all its fullness the initiative of love and the plan for true life that God has prepared for us. In Christ, *charity in truth* becomes the Face of his Person, a vocation for us to love our brothers and sisters in the truth of his plan. Indeed, he himself is the Truth (cf. Jn 14:6).

> Pope Benedict XVI, *Charity in Truth*
> (*Caritas in Veritate*), no. 1, 2009

The Law of the Gospel requires us to make the decisive choice between "the two ways" and to put into practice the words of the Lord. It is summed up in the *Golden Rule*, "Whatever you wish that men would do to you, do so to them; this is the law and the prophets" (Mt 7:12).

The entire Law of the Gospel is contained in the *"new commandment"* of Jesus, to love one another as he has loved us.

The New Law is called a *law of love* because it makes us act out of the love infused by the Holy Spirit, rather than from fear; a *law of grace*, because it confers the strength of grace to act, by means of faith and the sacraments; a *law of freedom*, because it sets us free from the ritual and juridical observances of the Old Law, inclines us to act spontaneously by the prompting of charity and, finally, lets us pass from the condition of a servant who "does not know what his master is doing" to that of a friend of Christ—"For all that I have heard from my Father I have made known to you" (Jn 15:15)—or even to the status of son and heir.

The evangelical counsels manifest the living fullness of charity, which is never satisfied with not giving more. They attest its vitality and call forth our spiritual readiness. The perfection of the New Law consists essentially in the precepts of love of God and neighbor. The counsels point out the more direct ways, the readier means, and are to be practiced in keeping with the vocation of each.

Catechism of the Catholic Church, nos. 1970, 1972, 1974

The principle of solidarity, also articulated in terms of "friendship" or "social charity," is a direct demand of human and Christian brotherhood.

An error, "today abundantly widespread, is disregard for the law of human solidarity and charity, dictated and imposed both by our common origin and by the equality in rational nature of all men, whatever nation they belong to. This law is sealed by the sacrifice of redemption offered by Jesus Christ on the altar of the Cross to his heavenly Father, on behalf of sinful humanity." (Pope Pius XII, *On the Unity of Human Society* [*Summi Pontificatus*], 1939)

Solidarity is manifested in the first place by the distribution of goods and remuneration for work. It also presupposes the effort for a more just social order where tensions are better able to be reduced and conflicts more readily settled by negotiation.

Socio-economic problems can be resolved only with the help of all the forms of solidarity: solidarity of the poor among themselves, between rich and poor, of workers among themselves, between employers and employees in a business, solidarity among nations and peoples. International solidarity is a requirement of the moral order; world peace depends in part upon this.

The virtue of solidarity goes beyond material goods. In spreading the spiritual goods of the faith, the Church has promoted, and often opened new paths for, the development of temporal goods as well. And so throughout the centuries has the Lord's saying been verified: "Seek first his kingdom and his righteousness, and all these things shall be yours as well" (Mt 6:33):

For two thousand years this sentiment has lived and endured in the soul of the Church, impelling souls then and now to the heroic charity of monastic farmers, liberators of slaves, healers of the sick, and messengers of faith, civilization, and science to all generations and all peoples for the sake of creating the social conditions capable of offering to everyone possible a life worthy of man and of a Christian. (Pope Pius XII, *Discourse*, June 1, 1941)

Catechism of the Catholic Church, nos. 1939–1942

A Proclamation Addressed to All

Acts 15:7–11

After much debate had taken place, Peter got up and said to them, "My brothers, you are well aware that from early days God made his choice among you that through my mouth the Gentiles would hear the word of the gospel and believe. And God, who knows the heart, bore witness by granting them the holy Spirit just as he did us. He made no distinction between us and them, for by faith he purified their hearts. Why, then, are you now putting God to the test by placing on the shoulders of the disciples a yoke that neither our ancestors nor we have been able to bear? On the contrary, we believe that we are saved through the grace of the Lord Jesus, in the same way as they."

For Deeper Reflection

One of the important ideas of the renewed impulse that the Second Vatican Council gave to evangelization is that of the universal call to holiness, which in itself concerns all Christians (cf. *Lumen Gentium*, nos. 39–42). The saints are the true actors in evangelization in all its expressions. In a special way they are even pioneers and bringers of the new evangelization: with their intercession and the example of lives attentive to the inspiration of the Holy Spirit, they show the beauty of the Gospel to those who are indifferent or even hostile, and they invite, as it were tepid believers, to live with the joy of faith, hope and charity, to rediscover the taste for the word of God and for the sacraments, especially for the bread of life, the Eucharist. Holy men and women bloom among the generous missionaries who announce the Good News to non-Christians, in the past in mission countries and now in any place where there are non-Christians. Holiness is not confined by cultural, social, political or religious barriers. Its language, that of love and truth, is understandable to all people of good will and it draws them to Jesus Christ, the inexhaustible source of new life.

Pope Benedict XVI, Homily for the Opening of the
Synod of Bishops, St. Peter's Square, October 7, 2012

— — — — — — — — — — — — — — — — — —

From the very beginning, the Lord Jesus "called to him men of his own choosing. . . . And he appointed twelve that they might be with him, and that he might send them forth to preach" (Mk 3:13; cf. Mt 10:1–42). Thus the apostles were the first members of the New Israel, and at the same time the beginning of the sacred hierarchy.

By His death and His resurrection the Lord completed once for all in Himself the mysteries of our salvation and of the renewal of all things. He had received all power in heaven and on earth (cf. Mt 28:18). Now, before He was taken up into heaven (cf. Acts 1:11), He founded His Church as the sacrament of salvation, and sent His apostles into all the world just as He Himself had been sent by His Father (cf. Jn 20:21). He gave them this command: "Go, therefore, and make disciples of all nations, baptizing them in the name of the Father, and of the Son, and of the Holy Spirit, teaching them to observe all that I have commanded you" (Mt 28:19 f.). "Go into the whole world; preach the gospel to every creature. He who believes and is baptized shall be saved, but he who does not believe shall be condemned" (Mk 16:15 f.).

Since then the duty has weighed upon the Church to spread the faith and the saving work of Christ. This duty exists not only in virtue of the express command which was inherited from the apostles by the order of bishops, assisted by priests and united with the successor of Peter and supreme shepherd of the Church. It exists also in virtue of that life which flows from Christ into His members: "From him the whole body (being closely joined and knit together through every joint of the system according to the functioning in due measure of each single part) derives its increase to the building up of itself in love" (Eph 4:16).

Second Vatican Council, *Decree on the*
Missionary Activity of the Church (*Ad Gentes Divinitus*), no. 5

BIBLIOGRAPHY

Brown, Raymond E. *Introduction to the New Testament.* New Haven, CT: Yale University Press, 1997.

———. *The Churches the Apostles Left Behind.* Ramsey, NJ: Paulist Press, 1984.

De Vaux, Roland. *Ancient Israel: Its Life and Instructions.* Translated by John McHugh. Grand Rapids, MI: Eerdmans, 1997.

Forte, Bruno. *To Follow You, Light of Life: Spiritual Exercises Preached Before John Paul II at the Vatican.* Translated by P. David Glenday. Grand Rapids, MI: Eerdmans, 2005.

Gerd, Theissen. *The Religion of the Earliest Churches: Creating a Symbolic World.* Translated by John Bowden. Norwich, UK: SCM Press, 1999.

The Greek-English New Testament, Nestle-Aland, 28th ed. Wheaton, IL: Crossway Books and Bibles, 2012.

Jeremias, Joachim. *The Sermon on the Mount.* Philadelphia: Fortress Press, 1963.

Laurentin, René. *The Truth of Christmas: Beyond the Myths—The Gospels of the Infancy of Christ.* Translated by Michael J. Wrenn. St. Petersham, MA: St. Bede's, 1982.

Leon-Dufour, Xavier, ed. *Dictionary of Biblical Theology.* Translated by E. M. Stewart. London: Geoffrey Chapman, 1973.

Martini, Carlo Maria. *The Gospel Way of Mary: A Journey of Trust and Surrender.* Translated by Marsha Daigle-Williamson. Frederick, MD: Word Among Us Press, 2011.

The New Jerusalem Bible. Ed. Henry Wansbrough. London: Darton, Longman, and Todd, 1990.

Sanders, Ed Parish. *Paul and Palestinian Judaism.* Philadelphia: Fortress Press, 1977.

Schürer, Emil. *A History of the Jewish People in the Time of Jesus Christ.* 5 vols. Peabody, MA: Hendrickson, 1994.

Maria Rosa Poggio has been involved in instruction about Christian culture and in the catechesis of young people for many years. Her pedagogical and teaching experiences are evident in her numerous successful publications for adolescents.

As a cultural anthropologist, she has advanced the study of the Letters of Paul in relation to the evangelical concept of "gift." She has also studied Christian communities in Brazil, conducting comprehensive research on strategies for social cohesion, cultural contamination, communication, and catechesis.

Libreria Editrice Vaticana has recently published her book on the faith as presented in the *Catechism of the Catholic Church* and her book on the Mysteries of the Rosary, both in Italian.